FROM THE FINGER LAKES

FROM THE FINGER LAKES

A Poetry Anthology

Peter Fortunato and Jack Hopper
editors

Cayuga Lake Books
Ithaca, New York

Cayuga Lake Books

Ithaca, NY USA
www.cayugalakebooks.com

From the Finger Lakes: A Poetry Anthology

First Printing – November 2016
ISBN: 978-1-68111-143-8
Library of Congress Control Number: 2016955266

Cover art by Mary Michael Shelley, *Ear to the Wind 2*
Copyright © 2016 Mary Michael Shelley
Pen and ink drawings by Ann Day

Printed in the U.S.A.

0   1   2   3   4   5   6   7   8   9   10   11   12

TABLE OF CONTENTS

INTRODUCTION

The Finger Lakes Region of New York is surprisingly difficult to define. Is it confined to the area immediately surrounding the largest of the lakes that everyone can see on a map? Is it delineated by the boundaries of 14 counties in the western portion of the state? Or is there something more intangible here, a spirit that can touch the human heart?

The editors of Cayuga Lake Books, based in Ithaca, cast our nets wide for this anthology, asking only that those who submitted work feel a connection to the region. We received hundreds of poems, and while trying to make the collection as inclusive as possible, our choices were often difficult. There is work here from writers of many different ages and backgrounds, some of them established poets, others relatively new to the craft, some of them presently living in the Finger Lakes, others who from afar recognize the region's continuing importance to them. We like to think that even those far away have its spirit with them.

The Finger Lakes inspire people in many ways to poetry and art. The waterfalls and stones, the hills and trees and wild flowers, the towns and towers and people etch their ways into the landscape of our souls—which is not to say that the poems in this anthology are limited to experiences about life in these settings. A poem can move easily among subjects and emotions, unrestricted by geographical borders.

The state of poetry in contemporary America is often debated and sometimes lamented by its critics. Hardly anyone can agree on what makes a poem good, let alone great, and it seems that no one believes poems are of much importance to the economy or to politics or to the entertainment industry—familiar obsessions of our society. Still, poetry and poets persist: we the people require poetry, and an astonishing poem or the sound of a singular voice has the power to rouse us from slumber. Reader, you will find a wide range of voices and contents and styles in *From the Finger Lakes: A Poetry Anthology*.

Dig in. Stay a while.

—The Editors

DIANE ACKERMAN

We Die

—for Carl Sagan

I

We die despite appointments and feuds,
while our toddler,
who recently learned to say No,
opens and shuts drawers
a hundred times a day
and our teen braces
for the rapids of romance.

We die despite the contracts
and business trips we planned,
when our desk is untidy,
despite a long list of things to do
which we keep simmering
like a pot of rich broth.

We die despite work we cherish,
marrying whom we love,
piling up a star-spangled fortune,
basking on a Riviera of fame,
and *achieving*, that human principle
with no known object.

II

Life is not fair, the old saw goes.
We know, we know, but the saw glides slow,
One faint rasp, and then at length another.
When you died, I felt its jagged teeth rip.
Small heartwounds opened and bled,
Closing as new ones opened ahead.
Horror welled, not from the how but the when.

You died at the top of your career,
happy, blessed by love, still young.
Playing by evolution's rules, you won:
prospered, bred, rose in your tribe,
did what the parent gods and society prized.

Yet it didn't save you, love or dough.
Even when it happens slow, it happens fast,
and then there's no tomorrow.
Time topples, the castle of cards collapses,
Thoughts melt, the subscription lapses.
What a waste of life we spend in asking,
In wish and worry and want and sorrow.

A tall man, you lie low, now and forever
Complete, your brilliant star eclipsed.
I remember our meeting, many gabfests ago,
at a crossroads of moment and mind.
In later years, touched by nostalgia,
I teased, "I knew you when
you were just a badly combed scientist."
With a grin, you added: "I knew you when
You were just a fledgling poet."

Lost friend, you taught me lessons
I longed to learn, and this final one I've learned
against my will: the one spoken in silence,
warning us to love hard and deep,
clutch dear ones tighter, ransom each day,
the horror lesson I saw out of the corner of my eye
but refused to believe until now: we die.

NICK ADMUSSEN

From Us and Back In

The spine of the mistake
we are making right now
is a slight ridge of blade
peaking up through the water.

It has been photographed and
faked, both many times; film
comes out grainy because it is
cunning and radioactive.

The waters roil, upend ships.

Maybe in one thousand years
a bus-long skeleton will wash ashore;

maybe they'll say what fools
to miss such a mistake
in so little water; maybe it's grown

feet already and walks in cities,

scratching out the record of its origin.

Poem that Drowns in Its Element

This is the poem that speaks
then unmakes what it made,
that apologizes for talking about itself,
that says black toad then looks
more carefully into the dusk and realizes
that something else is moving
along the bank of the lake.

The dusk moves on and there's no lake.
The year progresses and the house is gone,
its nights rented out to other tenants,
and can we say it is even the same poem,
now, stuck in a hotel room and afraid
to go outside because there's a fistfight
in the hallway, they're yelling

and there won't even be thinking
until the shouting subsides, it
subsides, so painfully fully that the poem
is dragged along with it. But getting dragged —
this poem has practiced it, it disappears
beneath the surface beneath the dusk:
purported amphibian, versed in dark water.

KAREN ALPHA

Waiting for the Family

We cross the bridge at the border of spring and summer
Every year as we mark it the anticipation
Of knowing begins, of yearning, and of waiting nearly over
All past years crowd back into this mind
The vision of them rippling like water over rocks
Until it becomes clear, the memory, and all the trees
Will part for water, rocks will rise up until
Tires jump the lip of the bridge and we ascend
Into steel framework, obscuring railings, flags
      the blip blip blip of seamed roadbed
           hanging in space

No one has mentioned it yet, however
The thought has minnowed and winnowed
From memory's neurons into the cortex of now
Because it must, because the combination
Of habit and pleasure demands it so
My head turns, your eyes slide left
I lift in the seat to peer over, just as we climb
The second bridge and automatically you say
Is it still there?
      Because of course it is
          And has been for 50 years

Some day we hope to see the occupants
Of Trois Isles, their grandchildren slipping into
Canoes, an uncle unloading cardboard boxes
Of groceries from the motor launch
A luncheon party gathered in chairs on the dock
All drinking from glasses whose dust was blown off
Just today just this morning as someone
Mixed the salad and ran rust from the watertap
But we have never glimpsed such sign of life
      boathouse doors lifted

floating canoe tied to cleat
paddle lying just there
Not once in all these flowing years
their fleet and shining
current.

BEN ALTMAN

Eyes Closed

One arm outstretched, a woman floats on air.
Her skirt, blown back, displays pale underwear.
If she knows, she doesn't seem to care.
The unknown people drinking coffee unaware

have heard the thud – this was years ago –
and are most likely dead themselves. Also
the photographer who got the shot. Although
his camera still exists, perhaps, who knows,

idle in some attic or collector's box.
This photo's from a book with little text –
five hundred photographers, one print each,
one impression, one attempt to catch

and frame. Most are gone. Short or long careers
alert for flesh and feathers, hair and fear,
arranging what they saw, changing what was there.
Now ink on paper. Indexed, page and year.

KATHERINE ANDERSON

Rush

As if he had materialized from nowhere or from
Main Street Willimantic circa 1973 reincarnated
Beautiful young man long blonde hair bearded
Plaid-shirt-wearing golden boy not one of those
Hipsters you see so many of these days but the
Real thing shimmering keeping pace a few steps
Ahead of me on the sidewalk right in front of the
William Henry Miller Inn as if he had dropped out
Of the blue step-danced from an apartment door
That hadn't been opened in thirty years requisite
Spider Plant in its macramé cradle paraphernalia
On a table Irish map Mad Magazine Jack Kerouac
There where I left off on the back stoop searching
For a long lost earring that must have slipped off
And hit the ground without a sound a silver hoop
I can no longer remember if I ever found though
Something pure or high-grade an effervescence
Of that first obsession love suffused me I was so
Happy to see one of them again the prototype if
Not the original dazzled sun falling all over him.

INGRID ARNESEN

Ithaca to Dubai

When you call me at the designated hour
every day, and I pick up
in time to answer, on the cheapest Nokia in the country,
After the 15 second time lag you say, "There you are"
You tell me you are on your way to the grocery store
Or to pay bills in person, or to pick up a check,
Or to mow the lawn, or that there's a heat wave
& and you took your morning coffee on the deck
in February, or that the Subaru finally died,
Or that you have a sore throat, or that you've plowed
half the driveway so far, or that it's Mother's Day
this Sunday, or that the neighbor napalmed
the cottonwoods on the edge of our property,
that you miss me, that the lawn needs mowing,
that the lawn mower's broke, that the peacocks are gone,
that you are on your way to the grocery store,
that my mother called, that you were fired,
that you miss me, that you are going to watch the Giants now,
that something will turn up, that you have finished the laundry,
while I look at the tallest building in the world from my low floor
studio, and report that workers periodically fall from the
         scaffolding,
that the metro stops in midair, that the World is on hold for now,
but the sidewalks are still polished marble, and the malls will
         always be open.

Norway 1959

I saw the clouds come all the way down
to touch the mountain across the valley
from my grandmother's house.
No one at home knew clouds could do this.

In the sinuous climb to the top of the world,
my sister would sing something childish
like *Row Your Boat* after we were done counting
oncoming cars and blue oncoming cars etc.

"Why am I me?" quivers. "Why not her?"
"What is the difference?" Why were we in the back seat
together in the family car, slithering on two lane roads,
shafts of light on the violent fjords?
Why did I speak a different language?
What had I missed? Why did my cousins eat apples whole, even
          the core?
And what would my mother say when I lost my sight,
          my own fault for staring too long at the eclipse.

MARK ASHTON

Saint Lucy's Eyes

When the soldier robbed her of her sight and life
But not her hymen or her faith, she became
The patron of the sightless, keeper of the light,
Unmasker of the daytime hours (says Donne)
And centerpiece of paintings beyond count.
In them this martyr is alive and well,
No hint of thumbs in bloody sockets,
Daggers through the throat or gore on gorgeous cloth.
Her name and fate are told in extra eyeballs
On a plate–lidless, whole, and staring,
With drizzled drops of blood the finishing touch.

Francesco del Cossa's Lucy stands demure
In red and black while a zephyr vortex
Swirls her dancing collar, curls, and laces.
Some idea elevates her eyebrows,
Tugs the corners of her lips, as under
Modest lowered lids she looks askance toward
What her left hand holds. It's not a plate:
A stem that forks to carry eyes in place
Of blossoms. Lidded, alert and focused,
They seem at times to peer through peepholes in
The gilded board. I like to think they're
Keeping an eye on us, making sure we
Spot the painter's wit. It looks like Lucy did.

JOHN BAILEY

Two Colors

Paris streets are cold in November
Shifting colors fade to grey and amber
Afternoon slides away
We walk along the lonely quai
Empty branches lace the edge of silent skies

Amber buildings stand along grey pavements
Silently the grey birds sit on amber casements
Grey skies make a roof above
Emptiness enclosing love
Like the river after rain our feelings rise

The earth is in your eyes so brown and deep
Winter is the silence of your sleep
Look and see how grey my eyes
Small spaces of November skies
We turn and watch the river flow deep and high

When darkness comes and makes all colors one
Mist dissolves distinctions and day is done
You and I two perfect lovers
Holding earth and sky together
In a dark and silent room will softly lie
Like two colors

Two Colors

Words and music by John Bailey

Freely

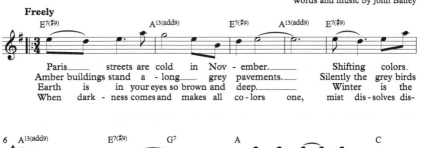

Paris____ streets are cold in Nov - ember.____ Shifting colors_
Amber buildings stand a - long____ grey pavements.__ Silently the grey birds
Earth is in your eyes so brown and deep._____ Winter is the
When dark - ness comes and makes all co - lors one, mist dis - solves dis-

fade to grey and am - ber.____ After - noon slides a - way.
sit on amber casements.____ Grey skies make a roof a - bove,
silence_ of your sleep._____ Look and see how grey my eyes,
tinctions and day is done. You and I two perfect lovers,

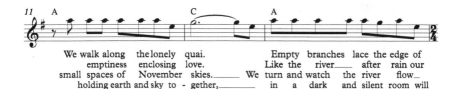

We walk along the lonely quai. Empty branches lace the edge of
emptiness enclosing love. Like the river____ after rain our
small spaces of November skies.____ We turn and watch the river flow_
holding earth and sky to - gether,_____ in a dark and silent room will

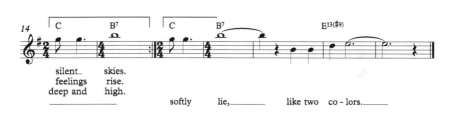

silent_ skies.
feelings rise.
deep and high.
_____ softly lie,____ like two co - lors.____

This lead sheet is scored for voice and guitar in the key of E,
somewhere in the space between major and minor. For a
recording of a piano version in the key of C visit
https://johnbailey2.bandcamp.com/releases

EMILY BENSON-SCOTT

The Problem with Paradise

From Key Largo, we drive down the great white spine
of the Overseas Highway, the ocean a gelatinous expanse
of turquoise, too improbable to be real,
lucid and orderly as an in-ground swimming pool.

Even the pelicans seem disappointed
their long faces exhausted by so many graceless landings
as they fumble through the air with the disastrous flair
of malfunctioning aircrafts.

Happiness is far more elusive than the easy paradise
promised by couples on honeymoon brochures;
it comes in bursts and flashes, like the nervous dash
of a neon green lizard across a slumbering gray rock

or a two-day train ride back to New York, with nothing but stale
       bread
and wine to sustain us, necks sore from sleeping in our seats
when I awake to find your black-fabric jacket
draped over my curled form like a cavernous tent of sleep

the vague reminder of your cologne
burrowed deep in the collar
the long tunnels of its sleeves
still lit with fleeting dreams.

JUDITH BERNAL

Immigrant

The enemy's hooves raise dust
across the plain. They are coming for us!
Quick, Father, into the cellar.
Throw your cloak over everyone.

We run to the river, hide in tall grass.
The horsemen ride thunderclouds.
I see a boot, a long knife.
We leave by night, horse and wagon,

village to village. January in the Ukraine.
Mother shakes me to keep me awake. We
cross moving borders. Land one country
claims Monday is another's by Tuesday noon.

Our village had twenty streets. In New York,
suddenly, a thousand times twenty.
I'm twelve, walk everywhere. That first year
I knit the old world into winter coats.

To My Son, on the Beginning of Chapter Two

It will start slow, so slow it hurts
        to wake up
when you don't know where to go,
        what to do first,
and you worry so, a dance with the dark
        that breaks all expectations,
affords no rhythm to count on. You are
        in the wind
and the wind blows soft and low.

You know how to dance: sometimes
       nothing matters but
how you keep your balance, that smooth
       low ride, air on your face
blowing you clean, electrons all aiming
       in one direction.
Good that you're in shape: it's good
       to be strong
when you take on the gods, easy to move
       when there's only one
road and all of you is on it.

Time's ticking, my son. All there is
       is what you have
and time, a simple multiplication.
       Behind the green door
the tiger's been let out and the other door
       leads to nowhere you know.
You'll find your face in the hall of mirrors
       next to your face,
just behind the door that's always opening.

BHISHAM BHERWANI

Horology

A tawny halo settles on the hill
over the student union and the chapel.
A path runs down
fifty yards
to a dorm, mine once.

The ancients used the stars
to estimate the hour
at night with astrolabes. I wear
a chronograph
with ambient hands and digits.

I wind
it every day but still it falls behind
some minutes.
Grandfather wore it
aligned to his forearm's underside.

I'm as old as it is.
Little changes
in twenty years: the buildings
in relief
against the sky, below the sun-

singed clouds
the quad
plum-rimmed, in the distance
the lilac iridescence
beyond the trees

around the cobalt lake spread like a sea,
are familiar.
The stone tower
with illuminated dial
will forever

stand here and do its thing
above and through the din.
The mechanical
clock's hands tick
and carve into halves

my years to date;
its face radiates;
and, resounding
from the chimes, the alma mater
rings.

PEGGY BILLINGS

Goodbye to the Bridegroom Tree

I watched you fall
      where you had stood
planted beside the Bridal Tree
      nearly two centuries ago.

The sawdust which rose
      from where you fell
rode the light drifting down
      covered the circles of your life.

It shone like the cosmic dust
      forming the rings of Saturn—
the remains of stars and broken moons.

RUSSELL BOURNE

Too Cold for Words

Too cold to snow, night scatters
Milky Way flakes, millions
making little impression,
lost conversations.

Too cold on earth, dim moon
yearns words to fit its tune.

Too cold for noise, white-
tailed deer snuffle snow
with nose, hoof before
leaping off through
muffled traffic.

The Agents

You wait, and out of thick distance
finally wing the mute swans,
altogether, as one skein,
as if enslaved,

       condemned never to sing their song,
       bound to bear their secrets on
       endlessly, flying beyond
       known horizons,

              perpetually white, urgent, and silent,
              blending with clouds, in and out
              of mist, long wings bent
              on Intelligence

JOHN BOWERS

Lucian Freud's Painting *Leigh Under the Skylight*

Brow furrowed, a dark stubble on upper lip
and chin, he gazes down in solitude
from his Olympian height, one massive hip
hidden by a huge hand, his attitude

defined by nakedness, by vulnerability
and pride, the giant trunk, poised in midair,
balancing on thick, elegant, balletically
crossed legs. From the brown triangle of pubic hair

between his thighs emerges, unashamed,
the penis. Light clothes the bare shoulders, chest,
the sagging breasts. The crown of the head, haloed,
floats high above the unrepentant flesh.

CORY BROWN

Autumn Lament

I lie in bed this morning with two poems in my lap: one a black
and white-striped clarity authored by sunlight slicing through the
blinds, perhaps its central image a zebra calf resting from a long
night of hiding from lions, or from very ambitious chimpanzees.
Or maybe it's a human ribcage laid bare and sprawled across me
like a lover, part of a skeleton the rest of which is ghostly and
barely visible, the skull on the pillow next to me, the boney feet
dangling off to the side, we two basking in a hot afternoon post-
coital high. The other is Richard Wilbur prattling about lilacs: "But
the sun suddenly/settled about them,/And green and grateful/they
grew, Healed in that hush/that hospital quiet." The first is
conspicuous in its silence and lovely odorlessness; the other's in
love with its own alliteration, a perfumed poetics. I myself am
weary of writing poems, a chicken pecking in the dust, for words
will never bring back my mother dead last month, nor did they for
her hers when she was five. What wafting scent words fail to
conjure anyway is worth the effort when it's death's smell we're
left with ever after? I don't mean the stink, though that reality was
true for eons before embalming, such that now we don't even get
that rank pleasure, the shock of knowing you're alive when
something you loved is not, the last gift of the dead. No, I'm
referring to a shock analogous to that one though opposing in its
truth: that since we are not in the end with anyone we are nothing,
wordless poems, blank and odorless images. But such a testament
flies in my face, for this is a poem, and for my mother no less, who
would've scoffed at such narcissistic nihilism. She herself dealt
with loss stoically, going about her days with an industrious
generosity that opened out from her as a force unstrained, like a
blue tulip, or a lilac.

Memento Mori

Sometimes when I read or hear a poem, I'll drift up and out—there
I go floating on the image of a raft down some mild whitewater,
trees and sky lifting me out of my petty anxieties, beer stashed
safely in the cooler. So when the cool purple-blue of a stove's pilot
light appeared in a poem I was listening to online, two sisters
doing dishes in its glow and whispering about a preemie born out
of wedlock, I was there, or here I should say, in my head, burnt
match in hand, my father teaching me to boil an egg. And in my
imagination I watched the match-head's smoke lift up like a snake
to the poem's flute music. Then that Holstein appeared, the one
that lay for three days with her uterus turned inside out out back of
the barn, a smoky purple-blue in the sky behind her, nothing to do
but stitch her up and hope she recovers but she doesn't. Then
comes her dead calf beside her, earlier, and then, finally, the
yellow tractor to dig a hole and shovel them both into it. That
happens sometimes too, the opposite of rising up and out.

JOSEPH BRUCHAC

Old Dance Caller

Standing at the edge of the crowd,
nondescript as someone head down
in a long unemployment line,
the music not yet started
and a younger voice behind
the mike on the stage above him
he holds his empty hands waist high
as if about to pick something up,
a newspaper, a book, a coat
to be swung around his thin shoulders
bent by the weighty hands of arthritis.

But then one foot begins to tap
the beat as the fiddler's bow
draws out that first note
and of all the partners
this song moves and honors
none are more true
than his heart
to this calling.

A Planter's Prayer

The Turkish poet Nazim Hikmet
wrote about the man who planted trees
knowing that he would not live
long enough to ever taste their fruit.

Perhaps I was not old enough
when I first read those words of his
to understand that sort of harvest
was also about the poems he wrote.

Now I pray, as he did, that what I plant
may continue to grow beyond my breath,
provide some sort of shelter for some
of those whose voices I'll never hear.

DAVID BURAK

Cautionary Tale

Giovanni, adopted son of Venitzia,
lost the lovely roof that had been
over his head for many years.

Some friends say a portion
of Gio's mind had drifted
into a sea of delusion.

As with many souls who
have been estranged
from reality as we know

it, & whom we see in
sidewalk tents behind
the Palace of Gold,

Giovanni was once a
prime attraction in the
Circus of Derangement.

He gained admirers
who whispered about
how Gio had entered

a state of altered
consciousness for more
than 1000 nights, with

only naps in the mornings
& afternoons. The diet of
this curly haired rebel son

consisted of dreams,
sunflower seeds, raisins
& homemade brownies.

He spent his nights
at The International
House of Mirrors,

gazing at images of
himself & others living
in utopian fantasies.

But one day, a respected
illusionist saw potential
& gave Gio another job

as a co-creator in the
Theater of Dreams, where
he lives in the loft for now.

MONTY CAMPBELL

Falafel

I looked at your ass in kung-fu grip yoga pants
while I was shaping falafel spheres and thinking about basketball,

I saw your lips shape a smile
in a radiant tomato slice with sea salt precipitation,

your low, luring voice was conversing with
caramelizing onions and perfect green grapes,

you observed my crooked hands prepare the purple cabbage,
you observed my crooked, scarred nose, like a nurse in love,
you observed my halo of lake clouds,
my coyote tracks for eyeballs
and rice follicles,

I unveiled to you,
the past,
present and
discontinuation of all invention,
due to the nature of hippie cereal and chocolate,

when I felt you cum,
the soul of the big red barn experienced alien fission,
I heard Zappa,
Peaches En Regalia,
toe curling purgatory
beneath the fattened stone moon,
night's cellular oil abandoning her human hosts...
near the bookshelf of contemporary poems,
action movies and empty, rectangular planter boxes,
near the lampshade of multicolored cloth shards,
the antlers of my brother's mighty hunting arrow,

the slow, maniacal burning of fluorescent green algae incense,

near the pulsating synapse that fires directly into the most animal
        portion of us,
the slice of us which smiles when our eyes open from dreams.

ALEX CHERTOK

The question

There were as many words for the smell of a train
just passed as there were in her mouth, just

alasness, the rattling sounds of leaving.

I was there, first period English, second chair
from the door, the day Ms. Dachs broke down,
choked up on the crockery breaking in her throat.

We watched her crack down the middle like a vase,
trying to hold it in behind her long desk.

Grown woman, wrongful grief, going through
a failure in her heart. I was seventeen.
I'd never gotten a speeding ticket.
I'd only seen this one country. To me

she was worse than naked. Naked would've stayed quiet.
She stammered as if her pants were pooled at her ankles,

beaten by both silence and speech, derelict teacher
without her dictionary, her eyes

staring through the back wall of the classroom
at either spindrift or snowfall, she couldn't tell
what was falling from what had already fallen.

Why? was all she said, over and over, *Why?*
climbing over itself before I'd ever

held a newborn. I'd never not
held my breath passing a graveyard. I'd never changed
a flat tire, or taken back a gift, never swallowed liquor yet.

I hated her that morning. I still bit my nails. I'd never
touched a woman's torso.
I'd never been in the dark inside

of a funeral home. I'd never licked the inside of a pomegranate
clean, or tasted sweetbreads, hadn't sneaked a look
at the cuts on a girl's wrist I knew
had been slit. I'd seen wind

from the inside of a bus make a wake
of a woman's scarf as she ran to catch it, but I'd never

yelled for the driver to stop, please stop.
I hadn't yet seen beets turn my piss bloody
or my brother turn ghostly on a throatful of kale.
I'd never sworn off something I loved

then clambered back to it begging forgiveness.

She must've longed to sleep
in that morning, in the warm room of that
morning, to hold her long life in her lap
and not leave the house. *Why?* of herself,

of the blurred world her body
had left the classroom to bring in,
of the books we'd read with no answers yet.

Essay prompt to end them all. *Why?* of us,
who never stood up, not once,
who let her cry alone.

THEA CLARKBERG

Home

The washing machine sloshes gently.
The house creaks, talking to itself.
Snow outside falls softly
Glistening with the stars in the moonlight
I sit by the fire
A slow deep breath in the quiet
Warmth in my toes and nose and fingertips
And a smile on my lips

Wild sky
Wild sun
Wild sea.
On wet sand
I stand still.

Whisper

With soft fur and godlessness
It creeps into your consciousness
With little mews
It delivers deadly news

With quiet padding paws
The Whisper spreads
With small piercing claws
The Whisper
shreds.

NANCY VIEIRA COUTO

Just When She Thought It Was Safe

> *Mark also the numerous land sharks who are on the watch*
> *the moment the young creatures turn into the bye streets*
> *that lead to their homes, to seize the opportunity to insult*
> *them, or engage them perhaps in conversation—and the*
> *result is ruin.*
> —*The New York Herald,* January 30, 1839

A convent girl, she knew the power of clean
thoughts and thought them, thumbed them like amulets
in the reticule of her mind. She was smocked
linen and cakes of soap until she saw

the land shark on the prowl with his white
teeth and whingding promises and splash
of isosceles handkerchief. He knew what girls
hide in their reticules. He had the advantage.

The land shark never comes empty handed.

Or so he says.

The land shark is friends with the girls from the Candygram
factory. He whispers, Oh nougat, oh toffee, in their ears,
Oh fudge, oh buttercream, oh jelly, into the curlicues of
their ears, his soft words nudging each honeyed cornucopia,
each sugared nautilus. The girls from the Candygram
factory make a map of flavors and shapes, rounded and
mounded and oblong and cherry filled. The land shark
doesn't like surprises.

The land shark schleps a tool for every emergency. Telephone
man, he says and talks a long line, a smooth line, a party
line. His voice is moist with anticipation. He has massaged

Pond's Cold Cream into his voice. His message has no
wrinkles.

The land shark is light fingered. He lifts an honest passion,
   polishes it, and buttons it inside his shirt pocket. Later he
   will pass it off as his own. He knows that the way to a girl's
   heart is through her passion.

The land shark's wallet is an accordion of membership. He is a
   Jacobin, a Jacobite, a jack-in-the-pulpit. He meets with the
   Carbonari in the soot-strewn back alleys of the night. He is
   a Tory, a Whig, a Teamster, a Wobbly, a scab. He has
   embezzled the dreams of a Rosicrucian, a transcendentalist,
   a clairvoyant, a seamstress, and a lady of Spain. He wishes
   they all could be California girls.

The land shark is playful. He sends his card with a message:
   Quand? Où? Combien? She forgets the nuns. She forgets
   mamma with her black shawl and her crystal salt cellar.
   She sends the boy back with her reply, framed in perfect
   penmanship: *Ce soir. Chez moi. Pour rien.* The letters are
   round and hopeful, only slightly slanted.

The land shark never leaves the table hungry.

Or so they say.

And what about her? Doesn't she like a tender
chop, a glass of wine, a blue-veined hunk
of Gorgonzola? Of course she sees the land
shark now for what he is, but it's too late,

she's ruined, she's ridden in his car-
tilaginous desires and learned a thing
or two about how a smart girl
can make it, as long as she's not particular.

ANN DAY

We Have Saved What We Can

Having only my arm, I hold the dog
to my chest, his heart beating against mine,
and put one book, a pencil, a scrap of paper
and a few smooth beach stones into my pocket.

Because I've been told I must, I have hung
my gas mask over my shoulder.

Everything else must be stored
in the fragile basket of the mind: the glint
of the dinner gong in the depths of the hall,
the black carpeted staircase rising in silence
past the glitter of red, blue, green light
from a stained glass window
on the landing;

one twilight with a single line of cows
following each other to the barn
for milking, and the faint hush
and slap of the tide rising and falling
beyond the window, slices of bread
held to the gas fire for toasting.

Seven decades later, I spread
these treasures before you, all that is left
of that life. Keep it safe.

Even the stones are important.

Old War

Ours is an old war now, ancient history
to my children
and my children's children
who find it hard to accept that once
real bombs fell on a dock
right after the children left,
and missed us.

Hard to imagine your mother
or grandmother, that white-haired
matriarch, leaving home
with a gas mask and little else
but stories of the island home
lost to invasion
by the hordes of Hitler.

Difficult to care about a life so nearly over,
a war fought so long ago
my father might well have ridden
into battle armored and on a horse,
or under sails
with orders issued
by Lord Nelson.

The names of men drowned off Narvik,
the weekend sailors
who crossed the Channel to lift
survivors from the waters off Dunkirk
are important only to those of us
who recognize the handwriting on cartons
in the attic labeled "The War."

SUSAN DEER CLOUD

You Are Driving North in November

After sunset
you are driving north
to Canandaigua
nothing but CD music
to keep you company
car heater
warming your legs
in dark stockings
while past windows
starless cold
cornfield stubble
a missed cornstalk
like a lone Indian staff
dead leaves
for eagle feathers
at field edges
trees like shadows
loom upright
in passing headlights
like corpses
the real shadows
you think
of flag-draped coffins
from Iraq
Afghanistan
not shown on TV
from another war
Crosby, Stills, Nash
& Young sing "Helpless"
car taillights ahead
red trails
floating over
old Indian paths

buried ancestors
"Helpless, Helpless"
you blink back tears
trying not to crash
into the twisting
shadows trying
to make a treaty
with this beautiful
loneliness

EDWARD A. DOUGHERTY

Lovers in the Lilacs
 — *after Chagall*

The beaked head turns from the bride's face,
bear paws sprout from the priest's wrists.
Look away and the shopkeeper
becomes a horse in gallop. On the tailor's soles,
another person stands, her head on the ground
as elegant and stable as a Greek column.

What appears to be agonizing cell splitting
is another form of union, what must happen
if we are to learn who we are in each other.

The lovers in the lilacs are lovers
and lilacs, fragrance on warm breezes.
And the moon is a pair of lovers,
never turned away, never far,
one face bright, one shaded.

Between dog and wolf, woman and man,
painter and peasant, earth and animal,
there is only the idea, the knife
that cuts going in and coming out.

The herring is fully fish and partly moon,
and the cow is what she is and is also the savior.
The dove bears a lighted candle
which does not gutter and will not darken.

Painter to the Moon

Mr. Z says he loves the stretching,
the preparing, the room like a dirigible

buoyant with oil smells and hand rags.
It has taken him years to learn

how a crescent shape whispers,
how one brush works like a bird's tongue

and another is a stone wall, dry laid.
When to go with which sensation, he goes by feel.

But despite all this, Mr. Z confesses:
I don't understand blue, don't feel it

in palm or fingertip, in systole or breath.
I use it so much because

blue is a question I keep asking.
He loves the hours that fly overhead

and are gone, schools of brilliant fish,
gone without us, entire in themselves.

EVELYN DUNCAN

At the Beach with My Fat Lover

Cargoed with flesh
he whales it to my raft
and I wrestle him on board.
While salt hills lap our feet
I cry, "More, more, more,"
shrill as gulls with a morsel.
Today, all our arcs and circles
praise whatever is full and round:
flesh, generous sky, plump sun.

The Butcher

Penned behind his windows,
he looks out at crowded aisles
where the luscious manager, high-class
as rolled ribs, elegant as
loin lamb chops, sometimes strolls,
her tender bosom capped with her name:
Loretta. He lifts his cleaver and
addresses the carcass on his block,
then wraps the parts in plastic
and sets them out like offered gifts.
Busy Loretta passes quickly, bites
into an apple, throws him a cool
smile.

GRAHAM DUNCAN

Chance Notes

Something hits the pane
two light, quick strokes
before it spins away,
notes not precise enough
to grace exactly Basie's
slow and tender blues
sounding in my ears
but close, so close.

I swivel just in time
to catch a glimpse
of chickadee, I think,
blur gone too soon to know
for sure, but this flawed
chiming of these tunes
(if two notes make a tune)
comes close to blending
nature's accidental music,
its casual way with pain,
and art's strict calling,
the two notes almost timed
just right by chance to grace
what Basie's music says about
the burdens that we share.

RYAN ELSENBECK

A Ballad for Syracuse

When rust became more than a surface
the people of no roots grew.
From the past they found no purpose,
their hearts: beaten through

trains and cages hastily made
from expectations built
but years ago laid
in withering lungs to wilt.

Most couldn't find God here,
only levers and gears half in the ground,
growing, reaching, and bridled with fear.
But the soft orange glow of my town—

like grass, so tame and wild,
breaking into cold salted pavement
silencing the lamenting exiled
from cries of false enslavement.

This place can rise like smoke.
This place will rise pumping
steel blood into a molten yolk.
And we will shed nothing.

DIANNE EMMICK

Shards

When I think back I know I must have heard
The sounds before my mind allowed them in,
And even then they slid back out so fast
They never registered as trouble signs.

Henry was sitting on the summer porch
And I was tending kitchen chores inside
When a CRACK! sliced the silence, startling me.
I looked up but Henry seemed unaware.

Calm returned. My unease slowly settled.
The world continued on its scheduled way.
But every now and then I'd hear a SNAP
Sometimes singly, sometimes in sudden bursts
Staccato groups of two or maybe three.

Henry dismissed a meaning to the noise.
When I raised my concern he shrugged it off,
Demanded lunch and dinner; life went on.
Serenity would follow for hours, days
And I'd be lulled into security

Until one day snaps and cracks cascaded
Upon each other, fireworks exploding,
Snap, crack, pop, pop -- and then a sudden thud.
A towering tree within our nearby woods
Fell sharply, shattering silence, sending
Its upper branches feet from our front steps

The echo seemed to strike against my heart.
I followed the trunk to the stump and found
The break uneven, stalagmites of wood,
Shards that stood ragged, sharp; they pierced the air
And then I understood the snaps I'd heard
And how the tree had reached its breaking point.

I glanced back towards the house and then I knew
I'd be leaving Henry at summer's end.

GENE ENDRES

In the Fall I Dreamed of Apples

In the fall I dreamed
Of apples, while stopped at the
Edge of the field, tasting
Sharp air and blue sky.
No more the fragrant blooms
Of spring. Instead, amazing tastes:
Alcohol—and the doctor's office
Or grapes and grapefruit
 "Plastic," she said, of that one.
Another tiny green one, looking like
An unripe tomato; hard as
Marble almost, and sour beyond
Belief. How can it be, we wonder
That the same fields give rise
To acres of goldenrod, looking all
The same, while two trees, ten feet
Apart, can grow some fruit
That looks and tastes as if
It came from two different worlds.

E. J. EVANS

Winter Solstice

After I was asked to leave I gathered up what I had
some crates of books my clothes a few pieces
of old furniture
I had a great weariness from the years of difficulty
and I gathered that up too
I did not know why I had these things
I was patient and methodical
packing everything into my pickup
moving with mincing steps on the icy driveway
taking great care with the arrangement
strapping everything down to the truck bed
in the darkness and the cold
with snow flurries making random sparkles in the air
and I pulled the truck out onto the road and drove
toward some other place
the road a straight line running between snowy fields
under a hazy sliver of moon in the starless dark
I knew I was to take myself and what I could of my life
and cross over into deep winter
I knew that in time I would pass through
and emerge somewhere carrying much less
and changed in ways I could not yet know.

Late Summer

You lay your life down as you go.
In fragments, and they are heavy
so you have to lay them down.
Sometimes you look back and wonder
what it is you have been making.
Eventually the work becomes lighter.

You find you can stand up straight.
You look around. You are on a terrace
overlooking a garden. The sun is getting low.
A row of trees makes a path to the sky.

DAN FINLAY

Going for a Ride

After fifty years
you still become
the stranger I'd like to seduce.

At loose ends this
summer afternoon
we go for a ride.

You enter the car
and swing your legs sideways
until your knees face forward,

and I remember the first time
you took your place
beside me in a car,

that excitement at the simple fact
of your presence alone
at my side

on the green seat
of an old Chevy
Bel Air—and I think

how old-fashioned
that name is, like us,
who would choose it

today when
Avalanche, Rogue,
Expedition

sell the allure
of driving something to
the top of a mesa

to leave it showroom
empty, which is not
what I have in mind

as I reach across the seat
to caress
the bare skin of your knee.

NANCY FLYNN

Meridian

Maybe you wanted to become
the sun, be noon, stand
on the threshold between
ante and *post*. Maybe you resolved
to straddle magnetic poles, mold
latitude from every veil wrapped
around your heart. How long before,
elastic knotted into a jungle of jump
rope that snapped then stung
the legs? Later came the celestial,
constant, every coordinate deemed
scribble then muck. Maybe you'd hoped for
a tooth of recognition, a dermis of float,
skein from salts, in the bath
one ellipsis inside a great-circle
symphony of wins or prepositions,
a cut-off pinky, saintly relic
resurrected within the lines
of longitude through St. Peter's
holy holy holy in Rome. How long
could you stand before the bullet-
proof glass and weep, one more son
marbled across his mother. Her gaze:
window on your midday, your own lost
count, the too many pulses past
ante and post.
On the threshold.
Your sun dallying.
Meridian.
Crossing at noon.

Tide Table

Leadbetter Point
Willapa National Wildlife Refuge, Washington

beyond the edge of words   a fading line
surrendered into silence   syntax   moved
directing where to stalk   or pantomime
in semaphores   the byways unimproved
beyond the edge of worlds   a failing dream
that seeks to beach   the tidal rising fast
past slipstream   rush through estuary   sea
runs eeling too   a salted push of grass
for refuge snowy   plovers   poised to lift
from mudflat nests gone boggy   skyward hail
upended   wintering down   a calling cliff
beyond the edge of worth   what loss unveils
inscription on the fly   leaf faithful   no
ellipses   still   how much I do not know

MICHAEL FOLDES

chroma

nick says the black and white photos work well.
that the black and white poems work well, too.
the long curving stairway up to his flat
gives him time to think, and stay in shape.
officially, it's the first day of spring.
when the warmer summer days arrive
nick will hike the Alps where the valleys
cannot be adequately described
in black and white. i wonder if it's true
what they say, that we don't dream
in color; but if you asked me the color
of the sweater you wore, or of the flowers
in the fields where we pitched the tent
roadside in the dark and awoke to an expanse
of goldenrod, i'd have no trouble describing it.
nick says the black and white photos work well;
we are not at all distracted by the purity of color.

the last wave

the wave didn't just roll in
it crashed onto the ledge of sand
rolled itself under, up, around again,
taking with it jellyfish and men
as if they existed in the weightlessness
of space, totally susceptible
to the suggestion of external forces.

the wave didn't just roll in
it boiled onto the short shore
bending and breaking backs

and necks, arms and legs,
embedding sand in teeth
like pave set in the nacre
of fastidiousness.

the wave didn't just boil in
it was a roiling wrench turning
nuts onto lightning bolts
that struck deep, reached
the depths of a black hole
opened wide like the mouth
of an angry, hungry god

with a thrashing head that
served its master no more.

PETER FORTUNATO

from **Letters to Tiohero**

Tiohero: the oldest name for what is now called Cayuga Lake:
"Lake of Clear Waters" or "Place of Rushes" to the native people.

3.

There's nothing to keep.
      Days I sat for the rain,
waited home
to clean kitchen, bedroom, bath (remember the music
          gusty wind out of the west
     rattling the window glass: inside of this
the busy dreamer is wakened
to the sound of gabbling trumpets
          flying overhead, the movement
of geese: clouds broke)
other times.
        Today the sun finally clearing,
burning off a light haze
I saw looking north—
          and I run to that
     down Head's hill into fox hollow.

    The nets I step into, half-aware, almost
catching myself at the moment:
was it looking out over these hills, Tiohero
thinking you exist outside of me
         as land or forest, the play
of light shafts in the sky;
was it virgin, wild peerlessness,
unattainable thought—you reflected beauty.

Why should the deep-lobed leaf of sugar maple
hold me so short a time?
      I let it fall,
               jogged on my way.
      Moving, I have tried to see
      the breadth of changes marked in landscape,
learned the flow of topo lines
expands the boundaries,
      meaning, here, these are your references
and travel where you will.
These are not your limits:
      men have gone into the ground at some point

and emerged.

Walking through the watershed of Six Mile Creek
      last spring in the evening,
      just darkening, but down off
Coddington Road I entered deeper shadows
below those hills.
         Poking around
         in the stone cavern beneath an old barn:
there's a tractor draped with rags, chains hanging
on the walls, buckets of rusty nails, paint cans,
forks and shovels leaning on a post.

What am I afraid of?
          —this intimacy grows
like moss on stacks of shale.
That was the way they built foundations
long ago: the hands of men
have held these things.

(The last Iroquois
      along Six Mile Creek
        pass away
     with the death of a leaf.

Some of those trees are pretty old down there.)

        Who did I see
bathing nude in the gorge,
washing her dogs, sunning dry
      on the rocky shore
      across from me (I whispered from the hemlocks
knowing I wouldn't be heard
above the rush of water.
Others have done this,
      passing softly through the duff
and paused perhaps
to notice those gaywings'
            purple crested lips.)

If I was hungry, I was fed,
but those terrible nights of blizzard
      you've got to keep moving to stay alive.

JON FRANKEL

Late November Light
—for Jack Eustis

The late November light is strong
It transfuses the empty arms of trees
And radiates the wooded land along
The shelves of shale crumbling free
Falling in a rush of silver drops
To the gorge below where everything stops.
Darkened by the shade, a frozen spring
In a caul of ice, enfolds the rock. Ice manacles
The fallen limbs with a shining ring.
Then the smoky violet panicles
Of grass shift in the sparrowed weeds
As Ophelia whispers of willows and reeds.

NICHOLAS FRIEDMAN

As Is

Just north of town, a quaint Sargasso Sea
for bric-a-brac: the barn, itself antique,
spills over with a grab-bag panoply
of outworn stock revalued as "unique."
Typewriters tall as headstones fill the loft
where they've been ricked away like sacks of grain;
a coffer yawns the must of oak—gone soft—
when one man, squinting, lifts the lid to feign
intrigue. Nearby, his wife surveys the smalls:
art deco bangles brash as harpsichords,
a glut of iron trivets, Christmas balls,
Depression glass and warping Ouija boards.
One man's junk is another's all the same.
They don't buy much, but that's not why they came.

The Illusionist

There is an art, he knows, to breaking down
the architecture of the make-believe:
    He must rehearse
    the concentrated frown,
the stuffing of each trick back up his sleeve,
    the *fiat* in reverse.

An unacknowledged master of thin air,
he swallows cigarettes and turns up queens
    while shoppers arc
    across the city square.
As evening comes, the thinning sunlight leans
    against the cobbled dark.

Like popcorn faltering, the crowd's applause
slows to a stop. Now for the final act,
    he packs his cases
    latch by latch, and draws
the tangled skeins of fiction back to fact.
    Still, disbelieving faces

goad him on, and—wanting more—demand
a deeper look inside his repertoire.
    His levities
    are merely sleight of hand,
but appearances alone will fill a jar.
    So, coin-eyed, he agrees.

Soon lamplight startles night back into day,
although imperfectly—the way belief
    at times inheres
    in what's half-hid away.
He turns the dove back to a handkerchief—
    then, grinning, disappears.

RONI FULLER

Persistence

You will persist in the *Asclepias*
along the throughway south of Syracuse,
in memories of challah, which I baked,
and which you would praise always as the best,
in thousands of my memories, alive
with all our joys and sorrows. Now I see
a smile, a gesture, now a flash of pain
across your face. Now I think how perfect
was the fit of our two different bodies,
how we would spoon ourselves when fast asleep.
I looked at and smelled that longing, sweet scent
of lindens in the city, now in bloom,
and heavy with a glory you would seek,
would revel in, revealing, without mask,
all that resided in you. Your own tree,
that linden I planted for you, now young,
but with its own blossoms, as sweet as wine,
as bitter as tears, stands alone, and I,
wanting only what I cannot have, smile.
There will not be a poem which describes
ineffable grief, or approaches death
and what it means to watch death, then survive.
And yet my curious nature forbids
distinctions such as these, and poems rise
to call me onward toward oblivion,
conjecture, and beauty. To say goodbye
is meaningless and futile. Spaniards say
that those departing go to god, but you,
persisting still, I have implanted here,
within the brain and muscles, in the bones
and so internalized I cannot say
adiós, for that would wrench, tear me away,
and I will not allow that vacancy,

that misery, that harshness of new loss
imposed upon the old. So you'll persist
in the tenuous fibers of my self
to make me rich beyond belief, and poor
as memories combine and fade and die.
To have lost you is my grief. Yet I loved,
knew you loved me—it had to be enough.

ALICE FULTON

Because We Never Practiced with the Escape Chamber

we had to read the instructions as we sank.
In a hand like carded lace. *Not nuclear warheads*
on the sea's floor nor the violet glow over the reactor
will outlive this sorrowful rhyme. Vain halo! My project
becalmed, I'll find I've built a monument
more passing than a breeze. It will cost us,
pobrecito. We can't buy a prayer. Did you call
my name or was that the floorboard
wheezing? These memories won't get any bigger,
will they? I think something is coming that will
vastly improve our quietude. I'm growing
snow crystals from vapor in anticipation and praying
for the velvet-cushioned kneeler that I need to pray.
I made this little sound for you to wait in.

Still World Nocturne

Listen, only night is watching the night nurse,
and her smoker's voice is not a voice I trust.

Yet I wake up and the world's still here—a blur

of how to speak or dress—which words or skirt
or pair of powdered, tear-resistant gloves.

Sisters, only night is watching the night nurse,

and no matter what we've heard, she's heard much worse—
the vacuum's roar, our mother crying Mother!

and asking if the world's still here—while versed

in flawed priorities, I numbly parse
a sweat of student essays, changing *is* to *was*.

Children, only night is watching the night nurse.

Tomorrow we'll confess all our concerns
about that villanelle's dumb rhymes on love.

We'll wake up to the world that's here—a burr

of sun stuck to a catheter's gold purse,
queasy music, wicked drugs. Still Mother,

only night will watch as I, the night nurse,

wake up to a world unhere, unyours.

MARY GARDNER

Home, again

The robin's back—
same spot upon the beam.
She builds her nest in a day or two,
nestles into it, stretches the weave
and waits, perhaps dreams.

Oh, the certainty of it all!
Lay a few eggs, keep them warm until
they break open and hatchlings appear.
Drop slippery worms into their open beaks
day after day, until your task is complete.
Then, show them how to spread their wings
and where the safe places, a kind of farewell.

I am comforted by her return, her trust in me,
the place I keep for her, as though it is a gift
to care for one another.

I scan this morning's news,
fret a little less about the day ahead.
I will glance up at the nest on the beam,
its tidy quiet, her head just above the rim,

and clean two rooms by noon.

CHRISTINE GELINEAU

Slieve League
County Donegal, Ireland

Cliffs draw us, as margins must: that limitless curiosity limits
      excite.
It's exactly the 600 meters of granite verticality that insinuates

closer, let me show you. Our thirst for clarity runs that deep.
The glittering little lake at Bunglass Point observes unblinking

as tourists and family groups head off along the ridge; there
at Amharc Mor, "the good view," a sketchy fence suggests

but well beyond, the man and boy stroll, and a girl sits leaned
against a stone, turning the pages to her book, rehearsing
      nonchalance.

This high up, the breathing of the sea is barely audible.
Watchers cross and re-cross the glass distance to the waves,

imagining the release, almost welcome in the manageable
summer air. Daydreams. Less than vapor. Assume instead

the composure of the heather. After the cliff walkers
return to their domestic suppers; after the noisome

cars reload and wend back, sunset stains the stones
mortal red and shadowed ambergris. In the mobile dark

of borderland the sea repeats without complaint
the siren song of its remorseless loyalty.

KATHLEEN GEMMELL

Tenants

They leave
such useless things behind.

Music you never want to hear
again. And clothes. Did they think
you'd want that faded shirt,
the color of old brick?
Notes from a life that moved elsewhere:
"Will be late. Sorry."
Books, and a fat jar
of Ovaltine.
A razor. A red toothbrush.
And junk you can't imagine
anyone would save: a cedar shingle,
scrawled on one side, "Happy Birthday, B."
Some present.

Sometimes you find something good:
A gold pocket watch with a delicate engraving of a bird
and a branch. A leather-bound book, mostly blank.
A fitted length of blue velvet—the stuff of dreams—
left hanging on the back of a door,
still in the long bag from a good store.

Someone should have that, wear it
to an evening soft with promise and desire,
someone still thin enough
and flushed—the color of that shirt—all the young-heart hopes
intact: Pleasegod don't let it end . . .

like this.
Nothing left
but doubleness and edge,
the litter of love, briefly tenant,
then gone.

The Domino Effect
Ithaca, NY: August 21, 1997

It was what they'll call a sweet accident
for years to come.
The guy really used his head
when the brakes failed
and the two-ton semi picked up speed
on the long, straight chute to the center of town:
Past the flat track houses on the edge,
one metal box moving fast through others going nowhere;
past the sloping lawns and Llenrock stone
of those who prospered and call this home;
past the large frame houses cut into quarters and more
for students passing through.

He knew the town. Knew the once brick road,
now asphalt slick, ended at the Commons,
a pedestrian mall,
where children played on the wooden gym,
hung by their knees, climbed ladders
and slid into sand;
where parents and others sat at cafes,
the chairs and tables of kindling or tin,
their bodies unprepared.

He called ahead, asked police to clear a path,
said he would turn wrong down the one-way fork
that fed the main road.
Turning wrong was the right thing to do.

Only one car slipped through the officers' net
and he brushed it aside as he took the turn,
deliberately sharp, rolled the truck on an island
between the roads, wheels left spinning in the air.

The cargo box split on impact
and 400 hundred-pound bags of the finest cane sugar
spilled over the road, the island, the banked earth above.
The driver walked away.
As huge shovels lifted scoop after scoop to the clean-up trucks,
people shook their heads.
That was one hell of a driver,
one sweet ending to the day.

MARY GILLILAND

The Bargain

I forgive the young doe for eating the blackeyed susans,
for hosta tops bitten just as the flowerheads formed.
So intelligent—she waited for the sweetest mouthfuls.

She's the first deer to stand, to let me sing to her.
A few brief chews, then she lifts her head like a bird,
walks off calmly into the woods after swallowing fallen pears.

This is a good house. We let out a milksnake curled in the
        basement
and moved in. Five years ago a stag browsed six-foot burdock.
Above their spikes antlers rose before he bolted.

The animals go before us, prints marking woods edge and trail
and the fair trade of the forest: lettuce and green beans.
Fence wire bends where cleft hooves sank, darkening moist loam.

When You're Away

Tasting you often, I seldom dream you
as a lover. With your good brown eyes,
you're the companion in the car
on a journey across the country or the past.
You must be filling the gas tank or
stopping for lunch when desire appears
as a tall woman who gives me
a drawing of a pig and turns
shapeless when I embrace her,
or a plump little man from India
to whom in my heat I cannot say a word.
Once I shocked myself: the lover was my mother.

But even she left, called away
and saying she'd be back.

These people hold their mystery
and I don't ask for it.
A rope pulls the world along with me
and it is not you.
You're a knot. I am.
I left some apples in the car. You
may find them before they freeze.

LAURA GLENN

Depth Perception

Last year,
walking this path,
wind blew through a pine tree—
for an instant I saw the ghost of the tree
made entirely of pollen, and shaped like a pine,
float through the air.

Something about this evening light:
distant streetlights cast long reflections
across the lake—shrouded, amber-tinted,
and shaped like upright bodies
bandaged by the light
like mummies,
though I also think: Ganges.

"It's the dead," I say
and start to cry.
"Father," I whisper.
I start to connect
to one of the reflections
—they're like cocoons—
as if something might emerge,
and my father and I might continue
things said and left unsaid,
heard and not heard.

Down the lake
of time, the reflections appear
in sequence—staggered—and stagnant
for the moment, like the gone.

My father loved travel—
India, Egypt, everywhere.
Where are you going now,
brave voyager?

As solid looking as the lamp lights' reflections,
reflections of car lights
move fast,
as if there's no one here
they need to stop and see.

I head home on my walk,
treading soft needles to humus.
My father, with his gift
for making something
of life, now is light on water: illumined;

swaddled, like a mummy,
about to start a new life . . .
and some part of me can't stop entertaining
thoughts I don't believe in.

JACK GOLDMAN

no longer burdened

no longer burdened
by the cares of containment
the empty bowl sings

under the streetlamp

under the streetlamp
my shadow hurries ahead…
i'd rather linger

my mirror reveals

my mirror reveals
an elderly stranger who
appears to know me

JOHN GRAU

Frederick, Maryland

I couldn't live in Frederick, Maryland.
Took a wrong exit on the way to D.C.,
getting my daughter moved.
Turned around at a middle school wedged
between an overstuffed residential area
and a clogged street overwhelmed
with Friday afternoon traffic—our meandering
maneuver no doubt picked up
on the school's security cameras.

I couldn't live in South Orange, New Jersey,
East or West, either—land of tiny,
snarly dogs made all the more testy,
no doubt, by lack of exercise and cramped genomes.
There's no left turns there and the diner
or store you want is always on the other
side of a lane barrier.

My next door neighbor lives so far
away that I'm only aware he's home
when he's sighting in his .308
or taking potshots with his Glock
at just-emptied beer cans.
Deer cross back and forth along
my road in herds, browsing their way
between corn fields and my old orchard.
Word has it that black bears are working
their way up from the other end
of Otisco Lake just down over the hill.
And, late on a hot summer night,
in the pool buck naked,

I contemplate this all gazing up
at the sequined scarf of the Milky Way
and listening to the warbling lament
of encroaching coyotes.

ANDREI GURUIANU

There is Fight in the Weather

It has been snowing
an endless morning
with little resistance.

If there's a message here
it comes *sub rosa,*
a contraband green,
Spring's suspicious offering.

Hours after signs
no longer point to anything,
sometimes the weary,
sometimes the ones
without any luck
look up without expecting much.

In a Burst of Silence

Find me ways to explode the monotonous winter blue.
Find me ways to live beneath the downpour.

In the canyon the lightning reaches for the earth with vengeance.
It craters the gap between here and now.

And the intimate lull that opens in a burst of silence.
That too is a way to cleave the shadow from itself.

Look for me then at the edge of what can't be articulated.
I'll be the one asking for rain, a dark, damaging wind.

THOMAS HALL

Han Shan in NYC

Greyhound from Boston to NYC
listening to Gary Snyder's version of Han Shan
riding down Adam Clayton Powell Ave
warm for November,
folks on street,
eating, sitting, talking, being,
Han Shan on Cold Mountain.
Also wondering what's happening at Zucotti Park.
Would Han Shan "occupy" wall street if in NYC?
or would he continue to occupy Cold Mountain?

PAUL HAMILL

from Notes from the Fifty-Mile Garage Sale

1. The Crawl

Late in July our Portobello Road
Is a country route that winds through peeled-paint crossings,
Gingerbread-house towns and a grand catharsis
Of repentant ownership. Upholstered monsters

Crawl from attics to die on the front lawns
By spidery farm machines, knickknack tables
And here and there a stand of church-lady pies.
Shoppers trudge Indian file along the roadside

As if a tribe had paused in mid-migration
To visit and savor its own spectacle.
Even sellers are swept up in the systole
And diastole of flowing bargains; lounging

Across to the neighbors, they bring home next year's junk.
And me? Suddenly inspired, must be dissuaded
From the drunken cat decanter, the miniature brilliance
Of a doll crib piled with doll-scale quilts. Such color

And whimsy spill from average houses
You'd think we live in secret carnivals
With rakish out-of fashion hats and bell-bottoms,
NASCAR loot, and whatever a skilled hand

At needle or scroll saw could metamorphose
Scraps of cloth or wood to over winters:
Quilts, whirligigs, ornate frames for Jesus
Or Elvis. We like the fancy of country crafts

But most love seeing what others have in the house,
Because for our own stuff our eyes grow drab

6. "Fresh"

Even with snakeskin, one can make an art
Of remnants: I asked the dealer in silver-buckled
Rattlesnake belts about shucked skin: he said
He gets his fresh because found skin's too brittle.
Here and there in the miles of yard sale tents
One sees a woman—it's usually a woman—
Selling things too new, like good men's suits
Or frames with recent pictures.   Her look
Is triumphant and grim at the same time.
I say to myself, "Oh, this snakeskin's fresh!"

LISA HARRIS

Extravagant Mercy

For every action there is a cost:
sensible things, limits, gushing love,
and all the grief of the world, a bitter frost.

She used almost a year's wages to buy
oil from India. She carried it in her waistband.
When he arrived, she doused his feet,
her hair a towel in a limited world.

For every action there is a cost
and a host of opinions about motives and truth.
Judgments are made and visions lost.

She lost her head and squandered the money,
forgetting boundaries and practical work.
Her heart ruled her head and she sang love,
and she sang forgiveness like the blues.

For every action there is a cost,
arise and arrive at pulsating grace,
and leave retaliation in the dust.

She broke open her heart to death
and let the sweetness pour out, second by second.
She smuggled infinity into the world,
multiplying zero with each breath.

ROGER HECHT

Witness Report

You couldn't tell distress
in the duck's face, not from
the distance we watched it.

Maybe in her gait, or in the rapid
turns of her head with the
traffic whizzing past. Certainly,

the raft of ducklings strung in a line
then rushing in behind her
showed, at the very least, confusion.

The duck hopped a granite curb
the ducklings couldn't leap.
It seemed a storybook tragedy

was playing out before us. A man
tried herding them to the sidewalk
waving off cars that slowed

& fortunately didn't wreck.
& when the ducks turned back
across the road, we knew

the resulting mess would form the stories
the dozen of us watching
helplessly from the gas station pumps

might tell our friends that night
at dinner or over drinks.
We're a sentimental town.

But all the lights were with them.
A woman lifted duckling after duckling
from the blacktop to the grass,

where the duck & brood regrouped
& could safely wander
to their certain deaths

sometime off in the future. & so
one by one we all drive off
with a great appreciation

of just what kind of world we have made.

Sky Burial

If only I could see
& smell, could
keep my senses
as I lose them
wouldn't I find it
delicious? The enzymes
without me replacing
the enzymes
within me replacing
cell by cell
my body. Patiently
they're waiting the day
my defenses
diminish, waiting
to transfigure.
& while I diminish
I will swell
like pride with gasses,
anticipating
my higher function:
protein for the cleansing

birds, a nest
my hair, my braincase
shelter for a mouse.
If I were any other
animal my skin
might become shoes,
my bones knives
or needles or buttons
or combs. It is fitting.
Nothing about me
wasted. Nothing
about me not becoming
something else.

ROALD HOFFMANN

Autumn Entelechies

1
The fever is past
but I feel fragile.
Like the Egyptian glass bottle of iridescent green,
        pasted together, but showing the cracks.
Like the Nabatean beads, peeling away sharp,
        onion-like, but corroded layers.
Like the old Coptic textile fragment, tattered
        and fading in all but its yellow and red.
I feel fragile.
My pieces are all there,
but they are held by weak ties.
My head feels the draft.
Mount me in the same museum case.
        Protect me from the wind.
                Arrange me and I will come to life again.

2
These are the days when the clouds
descend on our town. You see
them coming from our side.
The town is processed
by their passage, piecemeal
fabricated, pressed into existence.
Tree trunks made to be lost in the camouflage
of fall now just before the fog.
That yellow house wasn't there before!
The glen's cleft protrudes.
A two dimensional curtain
focuses a plane
by obliterating the background.
Then, against your mind's

ever-conservative
wish
to freeze
that scene,
while you scan
it changes.

3
Things have such difficulty
in becoming...The restless
blackbirds in the trees there,
what makes them so?
Too easy for the toolmaker
in me to zoom in, dissect, and
in the end (or at least
where I choose to stop)
adduce — neat molecules,
restive, stochastically
colliding to fabricate
the biochemical tinkerer's
tool kit, with it to assemble,
in sublime bondage
to the anarchy that drives,
things — as simply
laid out as microscopic
barbs on feathers, even
what is built into the chatter
of obscured birds.
                        But that
will not do. A purpose must be
externally organized; here
the hunter's gun, shot scattering,
reverberations — afeared,
in cawing disarray, they assail
the space newly cleared by the leaves,
are strewn to the sky...
only, in sweet time
to wheel into the flock
that we insist they be.

Speaker for the Dead
—in memory of Primo Levi

Shall this heap of gold teeth
pulled root and all by kapos
speak for them? They once bit
a sugar cube for every cup of tea
with raspberries. They remember
too many Sabbath sweets.

If not this, shall the unmuted
witness of man's base twist speak
of Mengeles and Ivans, freezing
experiments, the butt of a gun?
In the same camp a man
gave me two crusts of bread,
and some rare earth metal chips
sold well as flints.

Who shall speak for the dead?
I, said the dazzling southern day.
I waft you the smell of a favela.
I bring you news from a doctor.
And I, said my night. I give you
eels of comparison
with those who didn't come back.
I speak for the dead
when I take away your breath
when I wake you every day at 5
the time you woke in the camp.

ELIZABETH HOLMES

Red-Tails' Nest

Even when both the hawks are briefly gone,
eggs beginning to cool, this ragged wreath
of hemlock and weathered sticks is never still—

the variable wind endlessly combs and flutters
and combs the filmy, clinging scraps of down.

The female lands, wings wide over ermine
undergarments, princely ruffled leggings.
At once rocks her magnificent heavy body

into firm position over the eggs, and settles.
Talons folded harmless under, head
and hard eye droop, the whole body rounds

to the nest, her breast warms the speckled clutch.
But the wind will not settle; it parts the small
neck feathers to naked white under sienna,

burbles the lifting flight feathers' restless
round-tipped white, gray, buff, and leaves
unmoved only the rod-straight cinnamon tail.

The hawk is acquainted with stillness, though her feathers
shift and part, the stuff of the nest trembles,
at freezing dawn she nestles head under wing.

Like a trout in water she lives in wind. It isn't
a matter of accepting. The being *hawk* extends
not just to moving air but rain and cold, bloody

shreds of pigeon gulped, compulsion to sit

for weeks, neither patient nor not—god,
to have that oneness with one's life—

When her mate lands with his greeting gift
of a limp vole, she clamps it quick and flies.

Domestic

The night inside purrs with sleepers'
breaths and sighs, venerable
radiators' gentle clanking, a clock
picking its way past two. Curtains

nuzzle the windows. The broad sofa
settles, the cat nestles under its arm.
Awake, adrift, I'm the resting
pulse of this house, idling

in barest tinge of light, room to room,
at the front window widening
the curtains' gap. Two raccoons.

Black against asphalt's pewter
gleam, long-fingered hands
on bony arms pluck at a crushed
squirrel, guts protruding.

Arch-backed, feral, high
on their nimble toes they dance
and snap and snatch till one
seizes the squirrel in its jaws

and the dance is over. Carcass
swinging—flung over shoulder
an instant like a scarf—the pair
trot to the storm drain, crawl inside.

It all took twenty seconds.
The pavement's blank. Under a cloud-
encrusted moon, the bordering houses
roost, side by side, every
eyelid dark.

GAIL HOLST-WARHAFT

Why Should Birds Make Us Happy?

Why should birds make us happy?
Why smile at the house wren
scolding three sparrows close to her nest,
the great blue heron trailing its legs
like a long-handled spoon, the hawk resting
on a pillow of air, a Baltimore oriole's
burnt orange breast and a bluebird's cobalt
streak across damp grass?

Imagine the sky empty of birds
like a bookless house, a silent orchestra,
a planet without water, food without spice,
sea with no waves, a loveless life.
We've shrunk their woods, fouled their water
and still they come, singing, lofting,
serenely at ease in another element
as we can only be in dreams.

Cassandra's Babble

The old year ends, as usual, with Cassandra's babble;
        we pretend not to understand but it's not all Trojan to us.
Oceans rise, snow falls on palm trees, we freeze, roast
        and resolve to exercise more, eat less.

We fly far for the simple pleasure of riding
        a bicycle in the sun, and drive miles to walk
in the woods. We're all hypocrite readers
        of signs and portents, nodding at Cassandra's talk

and acting as we always have. Her lot
      is to waste her breath, ours to hear what we want
of her hoarse warnings, count the rest inimical
      to our way of life, a foreigner's panicked rant.

JACK HOPPER

Parking Lot Moment

He just sits in the car,
the radio on, with so much else to do.
Out there, the eternal shopping congregation
busily parking and moving in its pilgrim strides
toward the New Jerusalem of food.
The onion bagels will be gone,
The last shad roe filched,
bye-bye blueberry pie,
and the lines, the check-out lines so long…

But still he sits there, edgy,
unable to tell if it's late Mozart
or maybe Muzio Clementi—
that one sonata that he meant to buy.
Yes! "Clementi," confirms the announcer.
He turns off the ignition,
steels his heart for what's in store,
and shuffles with the others down the drive,
and through those doors
that always open by themselves.

Rafting the Medusa

My mother put me on a makeshift raft,
propelled us down a swollen creek,
our goal a distant highway bridge,
without considering how currents
often play one way. Along we floated
till the shadow of that overpass
darkened, and our fight to return began

as mother plied the pole
now upstream and against the flow.

The wooden raft's long dead,
and so is she, with mates of mine gone too.
I'm not alone, poling against the currents
on my own craft. I have drifted
down the river Alph,
conversed with Mr. Kurtz
about the horrors of one hundred years,
and am still unsure if I will ever
make it back against the flow,
the depth that's deepened,
the others clinging to our bark,
or recognize my place of first departure,
and who may be onshore,
waving us home.

ERIC MACHAN HOWD

Eviction

—for Michael

he was an island
when he came
third child of fear
first son screaming
upside-down, ankle-held
accepted
more Zeus than Icarus
and that first breath
smacked dreaming substance
from his mouth, nose, eyes,
to be buried with after-birth

stones

pull out the woman
rip off the thatch
and in the hole of home
throw stones to fill
the living
grieve island grieve
brother son friend
no roads to bridge blood

we sat in station
wagon, watched father
storm after storming son
into woods
storm after storm
twisting in the mind
pivoting on a father storm
under open sky

i sit on stone
the same which marked the end
of drunken nights
the same which lifted kisses to his weathered cheeks
the same which bore the splitting of wood
and now this heavy rock is buoyed by white gloves
unfaithful backs wedging in the entrance of my past
no man   no home   all fields of scattered stone

Atlantis, brother isle,
deep within some hidden
sea, you rise unseen
words choke
mouth full
smoothed stones
to swallow
one at
a time

RACHAEL IKINS

That Kind of Friends

Only you showed up 3 days in a row last September.
The heat, the 3 flights of stairs, weight,
furniture we lifted imprinted on our backs
arms, legs, my heart.

You unpacked the contents for my kitchen.
Lined spice bottles and glasses and a cupboard
rowed with mugs, plates for sandwiches and dinner.
You are that kind of friend,

who used topless Tupperware containers
to catalogue the cocoa, teas and baking
supplies, filed in easy-to-find groups.

A friend whose sentences I can finish
because, you explain, you're "an artist, not good with words,"
but my paint is language. You insist I "always know
just the right thing to say."

Almost a year after that September weekend
when I ended up in the emergency room, my heart
fluttering like a sparrow that batters against garage
windows blind to the open door, we head east
on the freeway in your Jeep. I ask,

"Where do you think my egg cups are?"
I eat eggs for the protein, forgot I had cups until this morning.
Painted Easter-egg stripes. Don't expect you to remember.

"They aren't on the shelves with the mugs.
Look on a shelf for oddities—juicer lid,
leaf-shaped nut bowls, a Russian tea glass."

After supper I climb on my step stool.
There they are, two left
from a 20-year-old
set. That kind of friends.

SARAH JEFFERIS

Modern Incubus

Like a night thief, you crowd
in my bed, already filled with Japanese
whining Sarah, *lay your sleeping*

head my love, human on my faithless arm,
and I have long since given up your skin,
your heavy wings.

In my arms, till break of day,
let the living creature lie, mortal, guilty.
On the line you demand

to know why I run over Jesus,
why I cannot let you be
you who will turn to river

dolphin during the day to bless and curse
those who ask for bread and wine,
you who framed my child self from bed to altar.

You, Beto, half siren will not basket me
to the River James. Not back to the Parkway:
the road marked with Indians.

Nothing is ever *entirely beautiful.*
Maybe *a pot, a rare bit of trees,*
a tall treasure, a told tray sure, a nail, a nail is unison.

I did not call you here Father,
across the oceans,
I did not want the closed stale

mate of a man promised to God,
a bird demon whose beak clips my own.

The Call

When I finally dialed, not drunk nor high,
it was worth the way you said, *Ahh Sarah.*

As if you were still my Abraham.
I cannot imagine your new windowless office.

Nor see my sixteen-year old self climb in,
stilettos and Chinese take-out in hand.

Oh the groups you must lead in basements
with instant coffee and stale donuts.

Do you tell them about me?
Do you confess my name?

Your name a kind of salt water taffy rotting teeth,
your name a boomerang I have been casting

beneath every other skeleton who entered mine.
Surely all of them were not named Michael.

The heart you say *has its own algebra.*
And I did love you, though it was all shrouded in—

In lies I say. I must have sounded like a ghost.
What can T.S. Eliot offer you now,

and after all those years of my lessons,
you still can't explain the resurrection.

There is no evening spread against the sky.
And my spine has risen off the table.

And the women, the beautiful women, my dear
Father lover, how I make them come and go.

MICHAEL JENNINGS

Trees

Today they've come back from the snow—
their dream-walk that began in December—
and are settling in along the ravine
where the creek runs, shaking the fatigue
from their bones, talking softly among themselves.
In a week the elders will speak in tongues.
In two they'll be chanting.
Muskrat will hum.
In a month the blue flower of the lake
will break from her icy spell.

Remains

My son guides me up the long hill
squelching in run-off, along trails
narrow as goat paths through the trees
to show me the strewn bones of a deer
nested in her shed shreds of fur,
almost golden, where some wood spirit
laid her to rest, and the coyotes
and crows stripped her, leaving only
a hoof and furred knuckle intact
among a clutter of collapsed ribs.
He shows me the clean white vertebrae,
the pelvis with its odd eye hole.
The knee still attached with some last rope
of sinew.
          This is his find, stumbled on
as he tried his new spring legs in a downhill,
helter-skelter run, and stopped, and stared,
and in his eleven year old mind knew

that this was the stuff of running
undone, something the receding snow
left for him personally, a sign
of winter's weight.
                              We eye it together.
We go down on our knees to gather pieces
of the witchcraft mystery. The gray trees
around us are also bones that click
and chatter in the wet wind
of almost spring. The brown limpid eyes
are gone. The crumbling gnarl
of spine, once nerved and tremulous,
is now only a train wreck the grass
will hide in a month's time. We feel
the doorway of earth opening.
We feel the thinness of our skins
and the prickling of short hairs rising.
We know what's at the bottom of things,
how soon the mayflies will be dancing
their measured reels of the evening.

ATIYAH JORDAN

a brown girl's nature poem

once i climb'd on my daddy's wide back/salt water wash'd the air
lift'd my nostrils/the first time daddy's feet w're shiny pearls/
commingl'd with dancin' weeds/ his knott'd skin broke off in folds
and stabb'd th' ground/o'er his scarr'd shoulder hangin' branches
took cool dips/ others wobbl'd in th' trickl'd wind/large humbl'd
steps still'd like black voices raptur'd in song/the river of glassy
green emeralds clutch'd onto his knees/ plummet'd against his
limbs as he climb'd/he let me glide my fingers between roots/and
thorns claw'd/i was invit'd to dance.

Tattoo

I got trees too I got birds too loud as jackhammers my birds
flower-hopping bees drunk on nectar yet those fruits half-peeled
acrid will be plastered beneath my skies sprung warm with growth
of wild cane there is joy in my jungle dust sweet free pasture of red
and black and brown clay its fresh rolling hills bruised blackberry
juice splashed across my canopy the strangest of fruits too belong
hung along these darkened pines and sun-dappled oak

JULIE KANE

The Ithaca Feminists' Quilt

Imagine the hours
sewn into this quilt!
Week by week,
the women's spines
drooped down to the curve
of a darning egg.
Sequins of blood
baubled and spangled
their fingertips.

At the exhibit,
men seem alarmed.
Stuffed like a codpiece,
a phallus
protrudes from each patch:
buttoned and ribboned
and balled,
risqué in black satin
and sassy in gingham
and prim in organdy
and serious in wool.
The men cluster and stare.

It's not the grudging
of time better spent
at charity or bridge,
nor their pity at anyone's
curling to sleep
beneath a blanket
of revenge; it's just
the nagging doubt
of what their wives

must talk about
at such a bee.

Love Poem for Jake and Ithaca

The bedroom window had a telescope
set up in front; but, other than that,
the room was a typical student's room:
over the bed, an American flag;
a bookcase made of cinderblocks.
There was only one book of poetry:
Comic Epitaphs from Country Graves.
I knew he wasn't the man for me,
though he always got up first to toss
our blue jeans on the space heater grille,
there being no heat in the upstairs rooms,
and sometimes he dressed me under the quilt.
I wanted to be a poetess,
pale, with a shock of copper hair,
drinking Jack Daniels on the rocks
and dying too young with love affairs
like Hollywood credits behind my name.
And so I crumpled paper up
and stubbed out Marlboros one by one
on the melting sides of a Styrofoam cup.
He always wanted to show me things
through the telescope: a white-tailed deer
in the field out back; a blizzard sky
into which the barn had disappeared.
I tried not to let my annoyance show.
Sometimes he strapped his snowshoes on.
I remember his lonely figure tracking
down the hill to the frozen pond
as I stood in the window tapping out
a line in my head with a cigarette.
I thought I had places to go alone.

If I could stand in that window again,
I would throw on my scarf and winter coat
and follow the trail of snowshoe tracks
past the barn and the glittering fields
to a world out of almanacs.

EMMA KARNES

for men

light breaks shame like criminal assembly;
my adultery a parade of livestock,
weighed/named/branded. this sunlight eats
at the open wounds of old synagogue facades,
pillaged once by mongering Romans,
twice more by starving Jews. *forget not
the martyred slaves* warns the moon to the
sun, but still it shines on my back.
like shame, a bright prison. famished,
lost in all holiness. even broken candles remember
the face of my twisted flirtation, my unshaped
suntan from falling asleep beneath the
circling sky.

I see my grandfather

In the reflection of the window grime I see my
grandfather crying real tears, his head rocking to
the shaking slaps of wind against thin walls. I
haven't spoken to him in years. In the gray of his
skin the clouds have furrowed even in summer, and
their rains have kept his feet heavy, stumbling. As
though he were the crumbling soil, he the air
humming of drought, he the stars disintegrating to
dawn; his jaw hangs in shame, his very lungs. How
are we to tell him? We must close the curtain,
touch his shoulders gently before he lurches away.
We must sing the name of his dead wife so softly
that he thinks it is merely the echo of her life.
Somehow, in the shoulderwidth of silent years,
I remember his rumbling voice, his thick stamp

collection from the tallest bookshelf. That distance is the nape of my body. That memory is the grime on the window.

DOUGLAS KEATING

Building a Bridge

Building a bridge from the smaller mind
to the larger one is no minor feat.
We begin by clearing the bracken and thinning the brush
along the banks of the stream
in some hitherto unknown part of the place.
The best spots to make the crossing
are usually not visited so often.
Tools and materials are necessary
along with something finer that we have collected.
Finally we come to our senses
and begin to work.
Sons and grandsons,
brothers and fathers,
journeymen all in this working
toward ever more human being.
And though the stream has been spanned
with strong timbers and solid stones
still a living wish is needed
to make the crossing
again and again.

KATHLEEN KRAMER

How can death be this beautiful, this cruel?

A tai-chi master,
with movements exquisite
and slow, the heron hunts.

His beak's a dagger the color
of sunset and his neck
a feathered serpent.

In the shallows, he stands,
legs thinner than stems
and sharply jointed.

He waits.

The hinge of his leg moves
and he lifts a foot, dripping,
places it forward one step.

Again, he waits.

Does he see the shadows
gliding beneath the surface,
Does he hear them?

Except for the flutter of feathers
at the back of his head,
he is a statue.

He strikes!
If you blinked,
you missed it.

Then you see the small fish
shimmering, quivering
in his beak.

He raises his head
and swallows—
once, twice, three times.

His throat undulates.
You see the desperate shape
of the fish slipping down.

Planting Wild Grapes

Every day at dawn I go down to the river,
fill my bucket to the brim and wash stones.
Big or small, I take all that come to hand,
dip them in my pail, rub them between my palms
and drop them back into the river. I listen
for the satisfying sound—the watery thunk—
as they settle among their fellows.

At mid-day I wade the waves of goldenrod
to the center of the sunny field behind the barn.
Beneath my feet, my shadow crouches,
small and black. The candle in my hand
stands tall, like me, its wick waiting for
the match, prepared to be proud of a flame
invisible in the noonday light.

Sunset finds me again at river's edge, a teacup
cradled in my hands. It holds rainwater caught
in the downpour at dinnertime. I lift it up
to the sinking sun, see the rim turn gold,
then tip the cup, spilling rain into the river.
Tomorrow, if I keep to my course,
there will be time to plant wild grapes.

C. KUBASTA

Forgive Us

In this too-long, too-cold winter
they tell us
to let the water trickle from the tap, all
day, all night, to keep pipes from freezing.

They tell us
we will not be charged for this trickle
that adds up minute after minute, day after
day; somehow, they will know which is water

we use; which wasted.

■

Old Croghan Man wore his skin over a tall frame, ate meat
often, yet dined last on cereal and milk. We think
he died in service to the land, a failed king.

Overkilled, bound with hazel withies, the bog body
nippleless, incapable
of kingship.

■

Forgive us, when we say things like, "he was not our [brother], our
        [people], our
[kin]." Forgive the way

definitions of family are contextual, the way
preservation changes based on acidity, temperature,
oxygen levels. The way
we mill around church luncheon tables of terrible food
nodding to banalities, making expected and unfunny jokes.

Forgive the way death leads to a loosening
of ties that should bind.

■

Last week, I came home to a flooded
street, ice-slicked, earth-moving equipment blocking lanes
and cross streets—no parking for blocks.

The water main by the hydrant burst and now

activated by danger, there is no way to prevent that freezing.

■

The local municipal authorities marked boundaries
with bodies, the bogs
preserved them.

We preserve our kin, by fire, by earth, by water—at the front of the
            church
the urn is sprinkled with holy water. The placing of the pall
is omitted. Cremains are not
to be scattered, or kept, or divided
as the body could not be scattered, or kept, or divided.

Except
that it can. I claim you as kin:

know what is used—what is wasted.

MICHELLE LEE

the thirteenth hour.

this is how quiet soliloquies sound in passive moonlight in church
light did you know did you hear how they set fires to their
whispers they lied they laid alone in ditches covered in debris
caught by the wind darling dearest did you think about the ones
who climb out with dirt under nails and cries caught in their
esophagi devoured by the insects crawling did you think they
would be foolish not be suspect did you hope they would be kind
what cause were you even fighting for you foolish fragile boy i
hope they devour you.

JAY LEEMING

The Barber

The barber is someone who creates
by taking away, like a writer
who owns only an eraser.
He is like a construction company

that begins with a large office building
and ends up with a small wooden house.
On the wall is his license,
showing that he's been to school

and learned of all the varieties
of loss. For this reason
a haircut can make me nervous;
sometimes I close my eyes

and hear only the snip
of the scissors, their two gleaming halves
talking of the balance that is here, the partnership
between this man in a blue smock

and the hairs faithful as rain,
that even before birth and after death
flow tirelessly out of the head
toward the comb and the blade.

River

The river leaves this valley
over and over, it has been leaving it
for thousands of years. A little trickling
among the rocks, a leaf swept away,
a branch slipped past a few stones.
And perhaps I too
am made only of departure, keys in my pocket
and name written in sand.
We stay by going. The river abandons
every place that it visits, and so remains there.

DAVID LEHMAN

May 15

If I write another
poem about Ithaca
let it be called
"Chance of a Shower"
no Korean restaurant
dispenses cherry
lime rickeys here
but if you bring
the white creme de
menthe I'll meet you
halfway with brandy
and make us stingers
you saw an osprey
a kingfisher two
red-tailed hawks
and four blue herons
in the Dryden wetlands
Renee you've become
quite a birdwatcher
and if a friend calls
and says "we've got
to talk" it can mean
one thing only you
haven't won the lottery

June 4

I said OK Joe what makes
this flower beautiful
what makes the flower
a flower he answered
right again as we walked
down Valentine Place past
the students and the nursing
home down the cobblestone
street leading to the bridge
above Six Mile Creek where
myrtle grows wild I wonder
why Milton said "ye myrtles
brown" when they're green with
little purple buds in May

STEPHEN LEWANDOWSKI

My Old Heart

Rocky highlands
south of here
are full of deer.
When roused at dusk
by a walker
they flee away
white tails held erect.
Long after their bodies
fade into the brush
you can follow
the flash & flare
of their tails
bounding away.

A woman who lives alone
high in sun rise and set
beside the highlands'
shady gullies and glens
can be chased but
will not be caught.
You would be a fool
to pursue her.

The Meadow

She wanted to show
me so we went
on a sort of road
through the trees
at its end and
into a recently mowed
meadow on top of the hill.
The mowing equipment
was parked silent nearby.
The sunset was brief,
pink and orange, the sky
too clear for much
color to last.
All the gone-to-seed
brambles,
goldenrod, asters
and Joe-pye
were lying down
smelling
wonderful.
The crickets sang
for the end
of the season
and their lives.
The spicy plants,
left-over warmth of sun
cricket song and
silence enclosed us.

DICK LOURIE

forgiving our fathers

maybe in a dream: he's in your power
you twist his arm but you're not sure it was
he that stole your money   you feel calmer
and you decide to let him go free

or he's the one (as in a dream of mine)
I must pull from the water but I never
knew it or wouldn't have done it until
I saw the street theater play so close up
I was moved to actions I'd never before taken

maybe for leaving us too often or
forever when we were little   maybe
for scaring us with unexpected rage
or making us nervous because there seemed
never to be any rage there at all

for marrying or not marrying our mothers
for divorcing or not divorcing our mothers
and shall we forgive them for their excesses
of warmth or coldness   shall we forgive them

for pushing or leaning for shutting doors
for speaking only through layers of cloth
or never speaking or never being silent

in our age or in theirs or in their deaths
saying it to them or not saying it—
if we forgive our fathers what is left

What It's Like Living in Ithaca New York

here's what it's like : let's say you have just had
lunch someplace in Collegetown and you are
on your way to Karl Yentz's garage with
your VW because yesterday you noticed the brakes were beginning
　　　　to fade

you start down the Buffalo Street hill　　it
looks like rain now after a sunny morning :
when you slow down for the blinking yellow
light at Stewart Avenue those brakes are
not good

　　　　and it gets worse　　that huge old green
house on the corner of Fountain Place and
then the shiny face of Terrace Hill Apartments
flash by you like the past　　you feel terror
in your wrists　　your stomach　　and you know
those brakes are gone and you won't be able
to stop at the red light on Aurora

where there are several people leisurely
crossing your path : maybe on their way from
the Unitarian Church to Hal's
Delicatessen or they just left their
own apartment to go buy some flowers
or whatever errands we do all day –
in any case there they are and you can't stop

so this is what it's like : as if your brakes
had failed and you couldn't avoid running
right through that crowd knocking them all apart –
panic　　broken limbs　　and screams in the streets

well the chances are that on any
given day at least one of these people
would be somebody you had quarreled with
last year and hadn't spoken to since　　or

a friend you had visited only last week
or even the person you once were married to yourself
who would see   just before the impact   that it was you
that's what it's like living in Ithaca

KATHARYN HOWD MACHAN

The Beets Poem

Beets: now there's a subject.
Dark red, rounded, hard as—
well, hard as beets.

I know a woman
who grew a garden last summer,
planted it with nothing
but lettuce and beets.
The lettuce didn't grow
but she had plenty of slugs
and beets, plenty of beets.
Now whenever anyone visits her
she takes them down cellar,
says, "See my beets?"
And there they are, pickled,
row after row of dark red jars
no one will ever open.

Someone else I know
always asks for beets, no matter
what kind of restaurant we're in.
Even at the beach
he'll go up to the hot dog stand.
"Got any beets?" he'll say.
And when the man at the grill
just stares at him, he sighs
and turns away, and spends
half an hour just gazing at the waves.

I know what you're thinking.
Why don't I introduce these friends,
have them both to dinner
one night, serve vegetarian?

It's not so easy.
Remember, beets is our subject,
and beets is what I hate about them both.

An Account of my Disappearances
—after Jack Anderson

1.
The day of roses.
The day of withered thorns.
With one small bag of paisley silk
I slipped into my small blue car
and drove, drove to Pennsylvania.
Shirts without buttons.
Quilts.

2.
Music gonged and hammered down the hill.
I stayed where I was.
No one saw me.

3.
The oven burned my cranberry muffins
before the priest could arrive.
I fled. New ice
shattered beneath my feet.

4.
The time of seven months.
The time I counted seagulls
like pennies in a fountain.
My mother had been dead
for many years, but still
I traveled South.

5.
Only my voice
like a nymph in a cave
ashamed of loving
a perfect man.

6.
The first time: to New York City.
With the boy I never saw again.
His name was Paul.

7.
The last one: raccoon tracks
in late Spring snow, daughter
of the one who growled and spit.
I put on my leather fox mask.
A red-winged blackbird called.

RUTH MAHR

Freedom Rider

Amy Goodman's voice
floats across air
so cold and wrung out
it's taut as a bow string

I'm sitting in my red,
salt-splashed, mud
splattered Corolla,
heater turned to high

and I'm cruising past
the stubbled corn where geese
carouse at dawn
honking like an 18 wheeler

in the west, soft purple's
rising from the valley floor
distant hills
shrouded in icy mist

and I want, I want so bad
just to keep on driving
straight for that purple
and never reach it

just keep on going, riding the cold
desert of this snow barren land
like the good lord said
leaving all that baggage behind

a snow flake flutters down now
melts a tear upon the glass

Willie Nelson's singing
Always on My Mind

as I ease up on the gas
and take the next left home

CAROLINE MANRING

Like an oyster opening

Happycakes, grimy brains,
you charm me into forgetting. We suffer

bouts of naming. Idiom makes nuisance &
we do not come when called.

Uninterpreted tree:
looks best dressed in dead, it's ok I promise.

Ricochets cause
wild love. No one says wild love.

Is your chimney up
to memory's standards?

Our beautiful intent to open
a series of cans?

You've made a filament, a fundament.
(How are these not just more lines?)

When you put two disagreeing words together
nothing happens. Something happens. A goose

stands up in the rain.

FRAN MARKOVER

Harmony

He learned his art on others' lawns, the ones
he mowed—blaze of dandelions, concentric
circles in a thousand grasses. But now he opens
his fence, walks carefully onto stones he placed,
imagines how a plover would make tracks in the
sand. Here he traverses mountain and cloud,
transcends father-in-law's pills, mother's heart,
his injured back. Here, rocks are bones, temples
for kittens who nap on lamb's ear and hide near
evergreens. The man steps toward the teahouse,
rising among topiaries, its carved-out moon
a crescent to secrets, a surround of pebbles
reminds him: befriend the emptiness. He plucks
debris with tweezers, the petals—water blossoms
offered to tearless sky.

Mother's Day

All day I've watched the common mergansers from my dock.
The female dunking her head for food, twelve babies skittering
in the lake to be near her. Once, five of her brood climbed
onto her back. The other seven trying to get on, slipping off,
trying again, the ducklings so close all of them travel as one
quivering body. I'll never know how she feels, what it's like
to be a mother, bear weight on my belly or back, feel skin soft
as down, wisps of hair stirring in the wind. I imagine if I did
have children, I'd insist that everyone be in tow, like moms
who rope their kids in a line when they cross an intersection.
I'd constantly look over my shoulder, holler to them, did you
bring an extra sweater, did you eat enough for dinner? I'd check
backpacks for homework, then at nighttime tuck everyone in

for story hour in our communal bed, clucking my approval
at least twelve times, sounding urgent comeback calls should
anyone disappear from the fold.

KATHERINE MAY

The Source

My fear had made its presence known
A drumming in my heart
No longer safe to shield myself
A life spent in the dark

Had comfort, had a little light
Could tolerate the tide
But deep within my sheltered soul
A loneliness of lies

A song began to resonate
A rescuing from God
Each note a solemn comfort from
His reservoir of Love

As fear withdrew and grace arrived
My legs began to stand
My voice attuned to harmony
Conceded to God's plan

One life is ours to contemplate
Superlative decree—
Eternal Now—a paradox
Both agony and dream

DAVID McALEAVEY

While holding obsidian from Milos

Other than what is before us,
the blank surface where these characters
figure themselves forth;

other than what surrounds us,
light in its diffractedness,
air moving through our throats;

other than the gift or trick
which connects us, makes this
one thing for each of us;

other than our differences
imperfectly parallel, mirrors
on opposite walls, receding;

other than our private histories
& other than the distantly inter-
locking histories of everybody;

other than the structure & form
of this message, other than a preference
for a thing this isn't,

other than our wish to be seduced,
than our wish to be first, to be
among the first; other than lust;

other than dreams, pools
whose colorful fish gaze up at us,
& other than any fear of death,

other than awe; other than the senses
careless of their youth
till they fail, & other than love,

other than friends ringed around,
firemen with a net
large as the horizon; and

other than the horizon; other
than moonlight; other than, on Earth,
prolific chromosomes;

other than catastrophe, & other
than the telephone, or the dual
tenacities of lichen & limestone,

other than our ability to imagine,
partially, paradise; other than
having lapsed as we neared the end;

other than another vision of the cosmos
& of time, & other than a plan
for mutual assistance: other than

a solution, other than a problem:
other than being born,
other than what we think.

Observing dusk at the Warren family camp on the shore of Lake Bonaparte, western edge of the Adirondacks

The lone skunk
nosing her prow
from cabin to
shed, boathouse,
lodge, peaceably cleaved

a slow arcing curve
around the aspen or birch
I leaned against.
Despite the streak
between her eyes
and the impressive wake
striping her body black,
white, black, white, black,
she was hugely calm.
Not happy: aware
of her competence.
She did not spray.
I may have flinched.
Any noise I made wasn't much,
the ripple of her passing.

JOYCE HOLMES McALLISTER

Pilgrim's Progress
(Beginning Journey)

I don't remember hawks and doves in 1948,
　　but there was an undercurrent of war in our house
　　　　as Dewey and Truman slugged it out to the beginning
　　　　　　of a bitter November and my father directed
　　　　　　　the campaign, leaning hard against his chair,
　　　　　　　　head tilted into the radio,

adding his own fifteen minutes of commentary
　　while Lowell Thomas repeated for the third time,
　　　　"Dewey leads down to the wire, a certain win."
　　　　　　Dad turned: *Maybe we'll get some sense back,*
　　　　　　　no more New Deal, no more Commies,
　　　　　　　　no more giveaways.

The next day was gloomy at our house. The newspapers
　　were filled with a gloating haberdasher and his round
　　　　spectacles and fedora hat. My father stopped talking.
　　　　　　My mother kept kneading bread dough, forming
　　　　　　　loaves all the same shape and size, uniform
　　　　　　　　perfect specimens in an imperfect world.

In the barn, our cows stood in their stanchions,
　　viewing white walls with placid eyes, chewing cuds
　　　　with silent detachment. They never worried about the
　　　　　　price of their milk, or bloody wars fought over grains
　　　　　　　that fed them, or even the endless bargaining
　　　　　　　　over the cost of their flesh.

things i can't write about

to feel what it is like
  to open the desk drawer,
    see the blank checks
      still in their box, unused,
        three years after your death.

to wash fresh spinach,
  suddenly taste vinegar on my tongue,
    remember how you sprinkled it
      over young cooked greens, and how i
      used only butter.

to see the shape of a car,
  maybe the same model, year,
    parked in front of our house,
      know someone else will step out,
      turn his back, walk away.

to stare at a collection of long slim
  notepads, read your name and address
    printed at the top in blue; on the bottom,
      thank you for your continued support
      of animal wild life.

my writing has always been more about
what I leave out, than what I put in.

KENNETH McCLANE

An Edge of Thanks

The snow is not yet a reality here:
and the first yawing of daisy, slightly overcome,
cannot be taken as a reckoning:

And though the wild-rose is gone,
the long-held rare song of a warbler
rises like a stairway:

Always, absently though irrepressibly,
this wintry world
wanders from the knife to the cross.

The Butterfly
— For my Mother and Father

See how the monarch butterfly
such a slight sliver of paper
ups and turns and ups:

How he seems so
oblivious to the steep staggerings of buildings
and the ruinous lights of the brook:

3000 miles to go
and wings so light
with going

BRIDGET MEEDS

I'm Ulaanbaatar

It's May I'm out of register
it's the cherry blossoms I'm quick and dirty
I need some means restriction
a mistake seen from afar
Maybe it's the lilacs I'm mindful sex
I'm back of the envelope I'm Pearl Square
I'm a baby near a boiling kettle
a tiger on a calendar
Could it be the apple tree I'm instamatic
I'm back of the house I'm your city's lake
There's restless agora within me boundless
I'm street antibiotic I'm Ulaanbaatar
It's May ferns forcing the forest floor
I'm an epidemic alphabet I'm your rabbit
the wind the rain the newly-opened window
it's very late I'm still awake   a door ajar

Sunset at the Office

Children yearn for mothers at sunset.
Your small voice on the phone is asking "when?"
My duties keep me here as of yet.

When sky darkens, I'm told you start to fret,
anxious to be back among your kin.
Children yearn for mothers at sunset.

Fiscal anchor of the family quartet,
I am looking at the clock again—
my duties keep me here as of yet.

My mother was a nurse at night and left,
a rustle of white in dark, to my chagrin.
Children yearn for mothers at sunset.

And then she died and I was left beset,
still needing her, a prayer without amen.
My duties keep me here as of yet.

Darling daughter, we'll soon meet for our duet
of bath and book and bed, chick and hen.
Mothers yearn for children at sunset.
My duties keep me here as of yet.

RAYMOND J. METRULIS

April

Ah! I am ashamed to be seen going to work!
why else be rising at daybreak
Yes, I am a poor poet in more ways than one
exploited by women they want nothing
but verses and swift romance
spring, my heart stricken as it should
and she has broken it off
like a blossom slipping from a bough
Joyless heart! woman without mercy
you have robbed me of fun this season
yet I have a sweet revenge
you could only get poetry out of this one
by leaving, so live forever

Leo Stonecutter

Leo Stonecutter
lives in the cemetery
self-imposed
he carves the stones

he places them over head
in the winter
his spade is hard
as the ground

in the spring
he plants trees
like everybody else
careful of earthworms

and talks aloud
leaving his cap at home

How Do I Say Free Beer in German?

how do I say free beer in German
well that's what's happening here

tonight dancing on tables
among artists and sailboaters

ah such a life my friends
my TV when will they hire

me to wash the dishes
singing the breakfast plates

resting with yellow gloves
on my chest at night

and that's what poetry is
glad and sad at

the same time
hold this poem close to you

the words get bigger

JERRY MIRSKIN

Rock and Water

They were a perfect pair.
The boy hunched over near the rocks.
His shadow moving gently on the surface
as if he were stirring the water.
When you looked closer, you could see
that he had something in his hand.
A small silver fish.
He was stroking it. Placing it in the water
in swimming position.
It floated to the surface and lay on its side.
Once, twice.
The sun shone on the side of the fish
and the boy continued.
Nearby another boy stood with a fishing pole
facing the other way.
He was busy and only looked over once in a while.
The boy continued trying to help the fish
by adjusting it in the water, placing it in motion.
Patiently and deliberately, as if placing the last piece
in a puzzle. As if it only needed a little help, a touch.
Once in a while the fish would actually stir on its own
and then it would slip to the surface as if having died again.
Each time the boy seemed more intent
and repeated his stroking, hovering like a guardian
repeating this ritual of patient affection and concern.
It was a very clear day. The water and the light glittered.
I stayed until I couldn't watch any longer.
Hovering as if to understand.
They were a perfect pair.
The little fish did not know how to go on living.
And the boy did not know how to let it go.

Seasonal Work

The field was bare and dry.
We stood up once an hour
to turn the sled at the end of the row.
The rest of the time we sat peacefully
carefully adding our bundles of grape shoots to the field.
The five of us telling stories,
what we liked to drink, how we spent last night.
The tractor moved slow as growth.
Four sitting, and the one standing
methodically placing another bundle in our laps.
The work was done mostly with the hands.
Sitting shoulder to shoulder
we pressed the earth between plow open
and plow close. Pressing
with our small fingers of life.

I think I remember that warm plow cut,
our four hands in the earth, putting in a word
and then another.
I think I remember our communal hands.
How they grew rough and dry as God's.
And how the driver called to us to *Go to planting*.
I remember that. His voice still hangs on a limb.

Seasonal work.
That was a good dream.
The next might be better, or worse.
Maybe next time I will have wings
and look down from above.
My hands no longer in the earth.

ROBERT MORGAN

Yellow

May is the yellow month. At this
latitude the woods are a fog of different
yellow-greens as first leaves
open pages and new twigs on the willows
grow bright as chicken fat.
In every yard the daffodils and dandelions,
and clouds of wild mustard light
the open fields, even as wind
bruises cowlicks in the rye. Along
highways and parks forsythia
sprays its heat, and fire rinses seedbeds
of old stalks at dark. The day begins
in a golden antiquity, flushing
the ridges so they echo inside the room
where flesh stretches into flower, where
even the interior of night is saffroned
the most erotic color of touch and know.

Purple Asters

In the months of lavender, late summer
and early fall, you notice the first purple
puffs on thistles, and out along
the creek and high banks of weeds the joe-pyes
lean like giraffes above the undergrowth
into tree level. Down by the branch, grass
darkens the same color Charlemagne had
his Irish scholars dye their pages for
jeweled lettering to play on like cities
in the desert sky. A purple butterfly
rolls its dice from chicory to burdock

to morning glory. And in the aging fields
ironweed opens bright fur to nectar moths.
Almost hidden at the edge of upland swamps,
lobelia and foxglove shake their sexual
pockets around bees. So much royalty
and ripeness! Foxgrapes fume the river woods,
and summer clots its ink in pokeberries
in the kingly time of sunsets and honey
trees and goldenrod. But all charge and color
are concentrated in this northern flower
the shade of the underworld and deep space
where stars begin, where the violent
and ultraviolet become seen dark.

BENJAMIN MUELLER

Memento Mori

The soil 'round here is about 80/20, mostly rock,
our neighbor informed us with a kind chuckle.

He had been watching us scrapping and wrenching
over the soil near the fence. We couldn't tell him

how we had prodded the earth around our house
for nearly an hour searching for the softest spot

in which to bury our cat. We simply smiled
as he drove off. We measured the dimensions

of the grave with our eyes, imaging how the body
might rest in it. And each in turn we stepped down

into the hole to pull rocks from their grip.
We laid the cat in his place— his body

having grown stiff with hours—
his head resting on a rock we couldn't free.

I couldn't help but hope that I would be buried
one day like this: No coffin, no service. Just a hole

in the yard and my loved ones placing each handful
of dirt and rock, a shroud that would keep my body

while life shuffles by offering a joke and a smile.
As my diggers chip away at the rocks, I'd rest

propped against the fence, chin to my chest, patient
for them to lay the shovels aside and tuck me in.

BECCA MYERS

The Raisin & The Bullet

practice by bringing your full attention

golden-copper

roll it between your fingers

rounded nose

what do you hear?

crackling?

if thoughts become intrusive

lifted, then dropped

physics of a dying star, red barn

iron sights assist

the parallel to childbirth

you worry it will hurt

place it in your mouth

expand and stop

soft enough to allow

the rifling's grip

now consider another

jacket first a cup

nourished by soil

a person drove the truck

returning from such wide-angle

remarkable journey

palms up

the present charts all sorts of action

aware of and perhaps

the approach, witness

in small groups on the floor

mothers leaning into diaries

the moment accounted for

of caliber, scene

equal to recoil

is mindfulness

ready: picture your baby

in memory

exit wound

ready: open
your eyes

HOWARD NELSON

Falcon Park

Minor league. Class A. Auburn Doubledays
vs. Hudson Valley Renegades. Very young guys
hoping to make it.
Small crowd. Maybe 500 tonight.
A perfect summer evening.

The Doubledays' shortstop is having a rough night.
He makes excellent stops, going right,
going left, but then
throws wide or high. One went into the stands.
Four errors, all throwing. He must feel terrible.

But his errant throws, and his suffering,
are not enough to keep me
from enjoying this cool July evening
in the stands, the crack of the bat,
the baseball ambience of well-being.

The pitchers throw hard.
How beautiful the swift passage of the ball
from mound to plate,
the emphatic firm simplicity
of the catcher catching.

Lots of contact tonight.
Not a lot of walks, or called strikes,
so the crack of the bat
echoes satisfactorily
through the night air often.

Line-drives. Also flyballs,
which suits me. I've always especially enjoyed
the way outfielders move, arrive standing waiting
for that long trajectory to come to them, to the precise
only spot of the glove in the whole spacious night.

Running catches a kind of ecstasy,
the amazing smoothness of loping and taking it out of the air,
or leaping, spearing the ball near the top of the fence—or
the ball out of reach, sailing above them
majestically over the wall.

So, a beautiful night for baseball—
and I like observing the fans
almost as much as the game.
A motley bunch, with our logos,
with our food and beer,

with our egos, our ballpark calm—
with our boredom punctuated by excitement,
pleasure of a good play. And the young couple
a couple of rows in front of me, with two little boys,
learning the atmosphere that will serve them well later,

and the way they seem to be happy together.
The husband and wife lean into each other
now and then, and he says something to her
into her long hair, into her ear, and she looks at him
and gives him an affectionate punch in the arm.

MARY BETH O'CONNOR

Fishing at night

The light draws insects and fry
which in turn summon larger fish
like the unfortunately named crappie.

You can lure them with a glow
stick or even phytoplankton in a jar,
get an LED that looks like it's bleeding,

or invest in fluorescent line
and a black light and a back-up
generator, headlamp, etc.

The lure of it must have to do
with darkness, privacy, stealth,
quiet skill

unlike when jacking deer, who are
not so much attracted as blinded,
stunned into catatonia, easy prey.

And with fish, you don't have to hide
in the woods and wait, your feet freezing,
or god forbid, track them.

Some say the fish want to be caught,
to fulfill their destiny on our plates.
Some say it's the sport of it, the battle!

Some say the fishermen secretly envy
the creature who can breathe under water,
like us before we were born.

STANLEY J. O'CONNOR

Disappearing Things

Pleasant Grove Cemetery in a winter
storm becomes a city of tall, thin towers
emerging like forest elephants from a mist

excessive, white, silent and immobile
snowdust making the spaces
between gravestones disappear

I can show you the past— traces,
fragments, distances, the lost edges
of inscriptions, unfocussed, out of intelligible

order, islands off the map,
names, dates, beloveds, prayers
reaching towards light and visibility

lines cut in granite dissolve like smoke
or a chalk drawing
in the damp and delicate air.

Light Years

before the shutter clicks
jane turns her head
to speak to nina who
is holding a plate of
duck paté and rice
crackers, someone's
hand, blurred in the
photograph, is reaching
across daphne but her

head turns away
she is watching toby
climbing a tree as
he always does for
parties, the leaves are lemon
yellow and they are falling
on the slate terrace
now it is beginning
to rain, slowly at first
we all get up and each of
us walks away into the
rain and the little
light that remains.

EDWARD ORMONDROYD

Pelican Requiem

Flop-wingèd diver dropped from his soaring
Into fish weather, deeper than herring.

Seagulls shrieked carrion

Salt and sand scoured him
Of web, lights and liver,
fish-pouch and feather.
Brainpan and keelbone remain of him only,
Sun-bleached and comely,
Shape-shifting in the light and shade
Of sloping sand above the tide.

Burly on-shore autumn winds
Tumble them and other ends—
Blackened wrack, sandpiper quill,
Crab claw, shards of moon snail shell—
Slow, slow aslant their demi-grave:
Slow spindrift on a slow dune wave.

Ghosts

The elm log in the fireplace warms us
with fifty summers of remembered sunlight.
Listen: the embers' soft hiss—ghosts
Of all those summers' cicadas singing.

A book of pressed flowers

These were vivid once as living eyes.
We picked them, who loved each other lip to lip
In the perishable world

TISH PEARLMAN

In the Distance

I sense a homesickness
for a place hidden inside my
marrow,
a lighthouse with the eyes
of my ancestors
longing for a glimpse of
land fall.
I know I have wandered
the lush fields of Ireland, and felt the spray
of the North Sea off the coast of The
Netherlands,
on the lookout for
a new world
in a time that does not
change.
I am homesick for a place
I never inhabited,
on a pilgrimage deep
inside the landscape of
stillness.
An age long past
sleeps in me, ghosting my skin.

ANNA PENSKY

I Know How to Trick the Immortal Man

Closeness—is a thought
The quartz oiliness of your forehead beaded
Up upon my chest—Unless
Give me no less, sister, harder,
I will be your only companion
Let my hand drive you to the reception
Let him take you home; but let me
Light the fat-carved candle.

Ah, they pass you!
Pass you like a crisp communion
A woven donation, circle, circle
Quick! Don't let them touch you
Dare I dance behind your back with matches
To peel away their gleaming rancid shadows
Little angel, wings of dough
They come for you with dripping mouths.

Oh, closeness—fingertips small
Meeting matching paradise paradoxic
Oh darling, all my life's been—Wrapped around your little finger
And please don't shake your palm in anguish
Yet wrap your hands around my spine as if
To throttle it and devein
What happiness I've yet to wrought.

I'd've loved to hand you to him
Watch his heart melt out like butter
And dribble down your chin.

STEPHEN POLESKIE

One More Time

If I could drive
yet one more time down the highway of my youth,
one hundred miles per hour, hoping that
some officer would dare to stop me.
Through towns with names like Nanty Glo,
where no one lives, but trucks take feed.
And Berwick, with its factory making tanks
for the military, which I refused to serve,
and the subway cars I later rode in my pinch-penny youth.
All day and all night long,
roaring along the river, that roars along the road.
And I, passing through for one more time,
my own Spring, Summer, and Fall.
But now my Winter comes,
and I move slowly.

Blue Sky

The blue sky is not a ceiling
that we can write upon with white chalk
but only a blue or gray or golden moment,
which records our passage through time.
These rare moments of closing
when things, like people,
come together only briefly,
fearful for those fleeting seconds
when they need one another.
The blue sky is not a ceiling.
The blue sky surrounds us always.
The blue sky reaches to the ground.
Passing but not touching

Meeting but not greeting
Looking but not seeing

LYNN POWELL

Love Poem from the Wrong Side of the Rain

What would April do? Tease hidden
meanings from the bulbs, raise the stakes
and double my entendres, and bet
all my roses on the bottom line.

But it's the season of embarrassed trees,
the modest charms of leaf-rot and briar
and hawk-scat thawing on the muddy path:
skinny March at an earnest latitude.

So tell me, muse: where around here might a woman
find a little flint and tinder,
some figure of feisty speech, a correlative for kisses
that would make a grown man weep if she put it
all on the table and headed out
for good into the long-stemmed rain?

July's Proverb

*The shortest distance between what's gone and what's to come
is you.* But that's neither here
nor there to the rabbit, plush
and quick in the rainsoft grass,
or to that taut bird, hotwired for song.

The noon sky acts as if nothing mauve has ever happened.
Clouds go on and on about the weather.
And soon enough, the delicate
hypocrisy of winter—snow falling all over itself
to wish you weren't here.

There's no wisdom in the windvane,
and no help in that daytime moon,
slow, half-hearted, besieged by blue. Yet the mind
keeps watching from its shade of words—
the mind and its archangel, the flesh.

In the Thin-lipped, Purifying Weather

Cold rain, zealous wind, and cobalt churned
to froth and whitewashed sky:
that's what an easy season always comes to.
The great lake hardens, its piers
reaching out into the deep for no good reason.
The sand comes clean.
And the park, that soft spot
for chess and Pabst and moonlit trysts,
gets overwrought with iron and clanged shut.

So who cares?
Nobody but me and that dog—
cruising the edge with a cold black nose, hungry
for a bit of sweet or grease, a skinny-haunched mutt
Caravaggio would have loved.
He whines at empty bins, sniffs
at the puzzle of gate and lock, digs in ground
that won't give an inch, till there's nothing to do but
hold up his head and head down the beach, the wind
so wild he trots a sideways jig
to aim himself straight—
our tracks a fugue of left and wrong and right.

FRANK W. ROBINSON

When I Had Trouble Sleeping

When I had trouble sleeping, she would come
And stretch out on me, above the blankets,
And breathe in rhythm. Soon I'd go to sleep
And feel at last, from beneath the covers,
Something huge pulling away from the bed,
As if my own heartbeat were leaving me.

Waiting in Line

I was waiting in line
when someone came up to me.
"I'm so impressed
with all you've done,
so many poems,
so many books,
so many people
who say nice things about you.
A little thin, of course,
when it comes to love.
But still… congratulations!"
And then I was next.

Dropping Sticks

Dropping sticks is a game
the summer crows have learned to
play, flying from May
to September, one above the other.
The higher lets his toy fall through the

air to the other of the pair,
who returns the favor. We gulp
to see these evening acrobats climb so
high, printed black against the sky
above the blacker hills.
They become absorbed in their little
game. It seems so tame:
one drops a stick, the other catches it,
what more is there to
say? Just that every day
my heart drops with it
through the empty air, till a strange
and gay and capricious bird, unknown to
men, catches that heart, and it soars again.

BERTHA ROGERS

Copper Beech Trees in Winter

Leaves arc, like paintings of blown leaves—
like cut paper, like sunset strewn
across red-gold sky, like smoldering fires.

Serrate-edged, notched, like some knives.
But they cut only the hard wind—
the wind that tries to bridge them.

Wind can't; these trees are too feisty—
they do not hide in niches or ditches—
they flaunt, they claim rough edges.

Farmers call beeches weeds—they push
through field soil. Their roots patiently wait,
shove worker-laid stones, open faces.

December disrupts, beats black branches,
feathered, fingered twigs—they're like pens
writing winter's aggregate history.

Black barriers. Hinged nodes above snow,
hanging on against blizzard breath—
hanging on all the scarred, bleak season.

The Pear Tree

Say that, while blading the plant-trench, you
saw leaves before they pushed out. As you
angled the sapling's feet into soil, booted
earth over roots, you tasted the fruit,
catalog's promise—years mere minutes.

This summit home, where you the living
try to thrive among stones exposed, deprived
of soil—this site wants five seasons before
it allows the tree fruit. Then, and at last,
the tree is pear-heavy—not the golden,
smooth, shining sugar you visioned—
but mottled, mildewed, misshapen eggs.

Say you, lost planter, watch while the deer,
the weather—reap ground-crop mush
among freezing fall, fungus-fingered leaves.

From the porch that holds your feet to
this home, you recall all the other children
you failed, every garden you let go.

DAN ROSENBERG

Best Friends

I'll give you my hair if you give me your skull.
I'll give you my feet if you give me your wheels.
I'll give you your face if you give me mine again.
What's owned in the world between us anyway.
A stomach that's been punched for your hunger.
My equanimity for just one fist flowering into hand.
Just one, friend. I'll open my eyes if you open.
I'll stay beside you if you. I'm unsexed and you
are the font of hunger. Your breasts keep time
with my breathing. Let's go to a show and you've
already seen it. Let's watch old movies and you're
a bristle cocked for adventure. You're a flea circus
and I'm a metal comb. I'm a rusty trampoline
and you're three small children. I'll play in you
if you play in me, the beloved. We'll never leave
the odd one out. In the dim exterior of love
we'll never leave him. You know the cold and I
know the cold, friend. I'll give you my blood
if you give me your blood. We can circulate
the blood between us. We will live forever you and I,
like stars we'll live. I'll orbit you if you orbit me.
Have my ears I'll hear with your tongue.
I'll shine on you if you glow back at me.
You give me your scars and I'll take them.
Have my hotel room I'll sleep in your cage.
Friend, turn out the light. Friend, the light.

HARRY ROSENBERG

Windblown

Near a hilltop bench
A peony troupe

White collars pink bonnets
Making curtsies, taking bows

To an endless curtain-call

The Clearing

I remember the last time I forgot something
But I can't remember what it was

And I forget the last time I remembered something
Or what that was

In other words, as they used to say,

I've cleared my head

CAROL RUBENSTEIN

Girl and Apple

The budding of the blood—ah, the green heart
high and merry in the body as hung on a branch
swinging on a white day.

Skeined with silky wind, the kicking heart's
secret dancing game is cloaked—
even from itself
stays hid
through long days and hours and long
nights of rush and whisper.

Ah, the red fruit is caught at last—all that wild knocking
by noon-sun traced
shadowless—this made
in steady buzz and drain of the true
summer, spelled
to a plumb-line.

In the gathered heat the unwinding of the sheath,
then the dropped solemn folds
about the feet,

awaiting from the new nude height
the letting go the fruit.

Ashen Makeup

The actors powder their faces with ashen snow to pass
        through terror, to enter a charged world, theater's sacred
                space.

Charnel house, doors-of-farce, any staged venue. Snow that
        mingles
        with whirled ash of human clay. Blood-memory chokes—
                spit it out!

Cries of Chorus unheeded by Players, scene coursing toward its
        end.
        Mid-syllable, the trap springs shut—Arena left littered,
                splattered.

What was and is this place? Crouching at the cave mouth
        to feed the guttering fire. Strike fear backwards, keep at
                bay

brute fangs! Cave drawings of our labyrinthine nature lunge
        in shuddering torchlight. Hands press to imprint: I, made,
                this.

How can sounds tell a thing befallen? How to stick-mark it
        to repeat? To kill before undone, to sing before turned
                stone.

Costume us with hide and feathers, we and they as one, switched at
        birth.
        Each season implacably instructs, blossoms its raging
                beauty.

Again the dancing god enters, greeting us—in turn we dance our
        greeting
        to the god—animal-headed, capturing brief time's beat.

No scene not enacted amid stage blood. Ragged shadows issue us
        with masks of changing roles, no double omitted.

What has claimed us for its unknown own? We who sing, we
        shaken
            back into stillness. Let this be told as done, redone,
                remembered.

Comes our turn to step past risk—unsayable
            utterance compelled: The one true thing that we must do.

Like particles of cindered smoke, like garments of an unknown fur
            thickening on the slain figures, flakes falling as must any
                snow.

LEENY SACK

(how I) remember antigone

knowing or not he was my brother
i was born to my father more than my mother
and though she self-impaled her dirty womb
squatting on someone's filthy sword (seneca),
that memory stays pale blood beside my own man's ripped out
       eyes.
i became his eyes, perhaps his sight, i like to think like manto -
teiresias' daughter - a seeing-eye daughter - visuality of exile

i am the chorus now listen
nothing so spectacular as man
or repetitive

if i could not bury my father my brother will do
any brother
again and again dirt on dirt and prayers to whom

my sister ismene survived
and the guard
survived

cry uncle cry uncle
creon creon you will die
not I
ever
my name will be sung and celebrated
yours forgotten or mispronounced

and from my virgin place infinite silk scarves
like from a magician's hat
will issue tales and tellings
interpretations and appropriations
moist or dry through centuries.

DAPHNE SOLÁ

We Are So Small

Fracturing the sky into lozenges of light
the trees stand silently
each one a black presence
just before the sun rises,
but it does not take long for them
to gather force and pride
in their own majesty,
march down the hill
to the shore of the lake,
and cross it
like Jesus Christ in full command.
Nothing can stop them
as they march up the hill
on the other side
and make their way across a continent.

No match for their life span,
at their feet.
we come and go,
come and go . . .
we are so small,
busy, possessed,
a spectrum of píccolo voices.
Perhaps in the highest branches
allowance must be made for larger souls,
Mozart trilling birdsong
Sappho and Virgil weaving incandescent lines
among the leaves,
and, on basest ground,
Stalin growling like a bear
as he carves hearts and livers
into a roughened trunk,

echoes and vibrations,
these and more should last forever,

but when dusk approaches
fading light barely illuminates
our darting figures,
overtaken by night
we are so small
so very small,
bearing tiny burdens
we come and go . . .
          and go.

WILLIAM STRATTON

Plenty, Hay

Much has been said already
on the subject of haying;
the chaff stuck to wrists,
blistered lines on the palm, the line
between red and white skin
where the sleeves of a torn shirt end;
none of these are revelations.
Revelations . . . And what did I expect?
To me, the heat was unbearable, the days
seemed to never end and the fields too,
immense and pitched on the side of hills;
my grandfather would lead a parade:
tractor, baler, wagon, and my long arms
reaching down with a hook
to snag the slowly birthed squares of dead grass—
I was tired of it even in the early hours
and by evening, having torn my arm
on a protruding piece of metal or
had the bald wagon tire bruise my thigh,
no feeling of great worth came over me
as the dark came over us.
I was less than sullen, but less than convinced too
of the value of such a thing—piling
five hundred or so bales
into the loft seemed to me just
a thing to do in order that my father
might hand me a few dollars
and leave me alone a short while.
Today though, I sat on the deck
and watched the spring wind toss
the pale leaves back and forth,
and smelled for the first time since August
cut grass and fumes and felt a little heat

on my face, and I was ashamed for myself,
to know that I had spent a few days
in the perfection of the world:
my body harvesting the wealth of the sun,
the dark earth, the water, the seed . . .
and I had not known what it was
when I was in it; something as pure
as I would ever know. Behind my house
the barn has tilted and fallen, the fields
mostly empty, my father gone, my grandfather
not far behind. I remember they kept a few
hives in the hedgerow, and the smell of honey
would rise above the clover and timothy,
the sounds of the bees coming back into tune
when the ring from the machinery faded,
the taste of it too, and the cold water we drank
right from the creek, so cold
you could only take so much.

SARAH SUTRO

Late

summer apples
   still hanging
   on the tree
dark red and brown
in the January dusk
grey day, a bit
of snow
apple trees
   branching
this way and
         that

pausing
   beneath the wet
   branches,
the north hill white
  and rocky

snow
landing
quiet,
white
veil
over
river

    *

memory of gold
  waves
  along the edge
  of seawater
again,
again

we went back
to find
what we had lost -
yet this kind
   of day -
   wave of gold and dusk
   out over
the snowy fields
what we
found is apples,
dark jewels

JUDY SWANN

Immaculate

After a few days the flower-crowded altar lists.
The lilies, not so white, reject the vase-water.

A yogini's straight spine is not common here,
where the faithful bow their heads or sprawl
on wooden pews, on hinged and padded kneelers.

A rough-faced man in his forties, a hunchback, and I
listen again to the story of the cripple healed by a word
and I root fervently for the cut flowers,
that by some miracle they bloom again.

CAROL WHITLOW

It was a gift (August 20, 2014)

Though I've long admired her beauty,
It was from afar,
Until one day
At my very doorstep
She stood
Announcing, "Here I am!"
And so she was, amongst the bright goldenrod
And courtly Queen Anne's lace,
One tall and proud magenta loosestrife.
"Invading", some might say,
I would say "gracing" my yard with her presence
We'll see, time will tell, if her charm becomes
Unmanageable
Which, I find,
A very special kind of charm—
Quite welcome at my humble home.

FRED A. WILCOX

Warnings

Down the road from Angkor Watt
Behind in front of stalls
It hardly matters
Huge white fish
Bargain, buy, and chatter
Gin and tonic moons
Clean cool comfy rooms
Descendants of kings and queens
The sweetest servants in the world
And you could almost swear
They mean it, but out in the streets
The children's bowls are filled with dust
Brown bag buggers cute as cocktail hour
Chablis and prawns and travelogues
While down the road from Angkor Watt
Specters grind black teeth
Like whisper storms, a silence
Deeper than bleached bones
 Children lick history from empty palms
And clouds wander dark and lonely
Across blind Khmer skies.

KIDD WILLIAMS

"Glides Smoothly for Effortless Writing"

If only you could fix that, little pen.
If only I could pay your $3.99, open you, put you
to paper, and find your slogan true: that it
now was effortless—that, after all this time,
the problem was really to write letters smoothly,
and not, say, one of selecting words, or staying
on topic, or locating the right simile, all of which now
are as hard as shepherding a group of third-graders
through a museum field-trip. If only the only
solution were to glide your tip over paper like
a figure-skater's blade over treacherous ice—
that is, ice marred by grooves and divots
of all the hacks who came before, but now
smoothed by your ministrations so that
I skate faster and faster in widening circles,
wind streaming through my almost-cobweb costume,
legs pumping and preparing to leap in a
dazzling axel that will make a little girl gasp the way
that none of the museum art did earlier, so that she
clutches tighter the wrapped roses she has brought,
ready to throw them down on the exacting ice
for me, just for me.

GREG WOOSTER

Enlightenment Abridged

Septic tank failure,
Cesspool collapse,
Filth across infertile ground.
Carried on the wind,
Seeds drop unseen,
Garden meadow blooms,
Senses pleased,
Truth understood,
Nothing more desired.

CONTRIBUTORS' NOTES

Diane Ackerman is the author of many works of poetry and nonfiction, including most recently *The Human Age: The World Shaped by Us,* which received P.E.N.'s 2015 Henry David Thoreau Nature Writing Award. Other distinctions include the John Burroughs Nature Award, Orion Book Award, Lavan Poetry prize, a D.Litt from Kenyon College, and being a finalist for the Pulitzer Prize and the National Book Award. www.dianeackerman.com

Nick Admussen grew up in St. Louis, Missouri, but his summers were spent in simulations of lake country—including a man-made lake outside of town intended to feel like the Ozarks without the long drive. It makes sense, then, that some of his work would take place at the lake's edge, that his first journal publication would be in the *Seneca Review*, and that he would end up a permanent resident of Ithaca, NY. www.nickadmussen.com

Karen Alpha lives in the southern Finger Lakes region, has hiked its hills, sailed its lakes, kayaked its streams, built a life. Her poems have appeared in several anthologies, including *Listening to Water: The Susquehanna Watershed Anthology* and *Knocking on the Silence: An Anthology of Poetry Inspired by The Finger Lakes.* Her own collections of poems, *All the Blue in the World* and *That Year on Blackberry Hill,* seem to find their subjects here as well.

Ben Altman is a visual artist who has lived in Danby, NY, since 2006. He has written poetry for much of his life, but has rarely published.

Katherine Lucas Anderson has lived in the Finger Lakes region for more than twenty-five years. In 2006, her limited edition chapbook *Greek Revival* was published by the Olive Branch Press and printed letterpress at the Wells Center for Book Arts. The poems have to do with the Finger Lakes, including "Hector," which tells the story of removal of the Native American tribes in the Finger Lakes from their ancestral home during the Revolutionary War.

Ingrid Arnesen first laid eyes on Lake Cayuga in the early seventies, and that was the beginning of a life-long connection to the Finger Lakes area. Today she again writes from Ithaca, having returned from Arizona via Abu Dhabi and Stockholm. For she always returns, whether from overseas or elsewhere, to see the slate remnants in the glacial beds, shards under clear water, her dear friends, and pine-studded ponds welded to the skies.

Mark Ashton moved to Ithaca in 1971 for graduate work at Cornell, and he and his family stayed after he completed his Ph.D. in architectural history. He has published scholarly studies in the history of painting and theory, and as a professional photographer provided illustrations for books on the history of architecture. He now works principally as an architectural designer. Some of his work can be seen at www.ashtonworks.com.

John Bailey is self-employed as a psychotherapist in Ithaca, NY, and has been writing, performing, and recording music since the 1970s, as a solo artist and with the bands Heartwood, Coconut Therapy, and Maplewood Jazz Team. He and his wife, the writer Holly Menino, established Deer Lick Farm in the town of Ovid in 1974, growing and selling produce for the Ithaca Farmers Market and other local outlets during the 1970s and 1980s. John's new album of original music—*All by My Not-So-Lonesome!*—can be found at BandCamp.com.

Emily Benson-Scott was born and raised in Ithaca and graduated from Cornell. She now lives in Brooklyn. Her poems have appeared in *Atlanta Review*, *Green Hills Literary Lantern*, *Cold Mountain Review*, *Nimrod*, and *Jewish Currents*. Her stories, book reviews, and travel writing have appeared in *Colorado Review*, *Postcards*, *Ultratravel*, and others. www.emilybensonscott.com

Judith Bernal has lived in Ithaca since 1977 and has raised her family here. Since she has retired, she leaves during the coldest months. Now her main connection to the Finger Lakes is through friends and a few leisure activities.

Bhisham Bherwani is the author of three poetry books, most recently *Life in Peacetime*. He is a graduate of Cornell University. Since 2009, when he received a Fellowship from the Saltonstall Foundation for the Arts, Bhisham, who lives in New York, has been a part-time resident in Ithaca.

Peggy Billings was born in McComb, Mississippi, in 1928. From 1952-63, she served as a missionary in war-torn South Korea. After her return to the United States in 1963, she went to work for the United Methodist

Church, devoting her life to racial justice, civil rights, community action, peace, international affairs, and women's issues. She has remained involved with Korea during its democracy and human rights struggles. She is currently retired and living near Trumansburg, NY.

Russell Bourne became associated with the Finger Lakes District when he married a woman who would not consider living elsewhere. They enjoyed the active local scene of hiking, sailing, and Riesling until her death in 2008. Since then, living at Kendal at Ithaca, he has gone on to enjoy the cultural strengths of the area; more specifically, the benefits of growing old and writing poetry in company with other artists in this engaging community.

John Bowers has lived and worked in Ithaca since 1970. He has published poems, reviews, and articles on poetry in *The Grapevine* and *The Bookpress*. He has also recently published a sequence of poems titled *One Year,* available online at amazon.com.

Cory Brown is the author of three books of poems, the latest from Cayuga Lake Books. His work has appeared in *Bomb, Nimrod, Postmodern Culture, Sentence,* and many others. He also publishes essays, which have appeared in *South Loop Review, Journal of Narrative Politics,* and *Autobiographical International Relations.* He moved to Ithaca in 1982 to attend Cornell's M.F.A. program. He lives in Trumansburg and teaches at Ithaca College.

Joseph Bruchac entered Cornell in 1960, graduating with a degree in English. He and his wife of 46 years, until her death in 2011, edited Greenfield Review Press. His first book, *Indian Mountain,* appeared in 1971, followed by his first collection of Native American tales, *Turkey Brother,* and five more books from the Crossing Press. He has also written a YA novel, S*keleton Man.* josephbruchac.com

David Burak's first poetry course was taught by Baxter Hathaway, founder of the Creative Writing Program at Cornell University. Many other teachers, including A. R. Ammons, Phyllis Janowitz, and Jim McConkey also provided him with substantive input on his way to an MFA in Creative Writing. His publications include *The Dualist, Not Loneliness* and *Celebration After the Discovery of a Premature Burial.* He teaches literature and creative writing at Santa Monica College.

Monty Campbell, Jr. is a member of the Cayuga Tribe of the Six Nations and lives in Seneca Falls, NY. He was raised on and around the Cattaraugus reservation and in Rochester, NY's inner city. Monty's poetry appears in such journals as *Spaces Lit Mag, Amerinda's Talking Stick, Yellow Medicine Review*; and in both volumes of Native American anthology *I Was Indian (Before Being Indian Was Cool)* His book, *A Large Dent in the Moon,* is a part of Foothills Publishing's Re-Matriation Chapbook Series of Indigenous Poetry.

Alex Chertok has work published or forthcoming in *Missouri Review, Cincinnati Review, Willow Springs, The Journal, Quarterly West, Copper Nickel,* and *Hayden's Ferry Review,* among others. He was awarded a fellowship to the Virginia Center for the Creative Arts, and completed his M.F.A. degree at Cornell University, where he was also a lecturer. He currently teaches at Ithaca College and through the Cornell Prison Education Program.

Thea Clarkberg was born in Ithaca, NY, and still lives in the house where she was born. She is 16 years old.

Nancy Vieira Couto is the author of a poetry collection, *The Face in the Water* (1990), and a chapbook, *Carlisle & the Common Accident* (2011). Her awards include two NEA fellowships and the 1989 Agnes Lynch Starrett Prize. She was born in New Bedford, MA, attended Bridgewater State College, and earned her M.F.A. from Cornell University. She lives in Ithaca, New York, and is poetry editor of *Epoch.*

Ann Day was born in 1927 in Malta where her father was stationed in the British Royal Navy. She spent her summers and the first years of the war on the Channel Island of Jersey, and came to America in 1940 with some 400 refugee children. A watercolorist as well as a poet, she has exhibited widely, and was Curator of Education at the Utah Museum of Fine Arts. She lives in Trumansburg, NY. *We Have Saved What We Can* is from by Cayuga Lake Books. annday.net.

Susan Deer Cloud lived, wrote, and taught in Binghamton for over four decades. She is a mixed lineage Turtle Island Indian with Mohawk and some Seneca background, so living in the Southern Tier became of immense significance to her because countless Native people once parleyed there. For a long time she lived not too far from the confluence of the Chenango and Susquehanna Rivers, an immensely powerful place for someone like herself. She now lives where she grew up in the Catskill Mountains.

Edward A. Dougherty first visited the region as a college student on a retreat at the Benedictine Monastery near Elmira, NY. After serving as a volunteer for peace in Hiroshima, he worked at Elmira College in 1996, then began teaching English at Corning Community College. His books include *House of Green Water*, in which he tried to give back some of his affection for the area's natural and cultural history. *Grace Street: Poems* appeared in 2016 from Cayuga Lake Books.

Evelyn Duncan's poems have been published in *Big City Lit, The Comstock Review, Phoebe, The New Yorker,* and *The Second Word Thursdays Anthology.* A chapbook of thirty-three poems, *Picking Up* was published in 2008 by Bright Hill Press. She has lived in Ithaca for the last fifteen years.

Graham Duncan has published more than 500 poems in literary periodicals. He has two chapbooks of poetry, *The Mapreader* (1987) and *Stone Circles* (1992), and in 2002, Bright Hill Press published his collection *Every Infant's Blood: New and Selected Poems.* He earned an advanced degree from Cornell University in 1953 and has lived in Ithaca for fifteen years.

Ryan Elsenbeck grew up in Syracuse and studied poetry with Dan Rosenberg at Wells College in Aurora. Like many other 23-year-old recent grads in the area, he can't say he will be here for the rest of his life because he's still looking for work. But the truth is, he wishes he could. He loves the long winters, the geese, the welcomed summers, the striking autumns, and his family. All these influence his poetry greatly, and not just in his poems that directly address the rust belt.

Dianne Emmick is a resident of Camillus, NY, and a retired English teacher and Department Chair at West Genesee High School in Camillus. She is a member of the Finger Lakes Writers Group that meets in Skaneateles, NY.

Gene Endres has lived near Cayuga Lake (Trumansburg, Enfield, and Ithaca) since 1973. He has never had any poetry published, but is a member of the Buck Hill Poets group, who meet to share their work and develop it further. Gene worked in multiple occupations ranging from high school physics teacher to broadcast engineer to grape pruner. He is currently retired from work at Ithaca College and lives in downtown Ithaca.

E. J. Evans lived in Ithaca, New York, from 1992 to 2012, having moved here from Panama City, Florida. It was soon after moving to Ithaca that he took a poetry workshop that inspired him to commit himself to the serious pursuit of the craft of poetry writing. He moved to Cazenovia, New York, in 2012, but he maintains ties, personal and artistic, to the Ithaca area. His most recent book is *Meet Me in the Distance.*

Dan Finlay has lived in Ithaca since 1966 and has worked as a teacher, a photographer, a social worker, and peace activist.

Nancy Flynn grew up in northeastern Pennsylvania, spent many years on a downtown creek in Ithaca, New York, and now lives in Portland, Oregon. She attended Oberlin, Cornell, and has an M.A. in English from SUNY/Binghamton. A former university administrator, she has received an Oregon Literary Fellowship and the James Jones First Novel Fellowship. Her poetry collection, *Every Door Recklessly Ajar* (Cayuga Lake Books), appeared in 2015; Anchor & Plume Press published her *Great Hunger*, in March 2016. www.nancyflynn.com.

Michael Foldes is originally from Endwell. He and his wife moved upstate from New York City in 1980 to raise a family and have been here ever since. He is currently manager for a manufacturer of medical displays and video signal management equipment for Healthcare. In his spare time he writes and publishes the online arts journal Ragazine.CC. His poetry, essays and reviews have appeared widely in English, some in translation into Hungarian, Romanian, and French.

Peter Fortunato's most recent book is *Late Morning: New and Selected Poems* (Cayuga Lake Books, 2013). A poet, teacher, visual artist, performer, ceremony maker, and hypnotherapist, he has lived in Ithaca for most his life. *Letters to Tiohero* was originally published as a book length poem by the Grapevine Press in 1977. Forthcoming from Cayuga Lake Books in 2017 is his collection *Entering the Mountain*. www.peterfortunato.wordpress.com.

Jon Frankel moved to Ithaca in 1988 because his family, including two babies, could no longer afford Manhattan. An old friend was at Cornell for grad school. Jon never intended to stay, but he has raised five children in Ithaca and worked in Olin Library for 25 years. He and his family live on South Hill.

Nicholas Friedman was born and raised in Syracuse and spent his summers on Otisco Lake. He received an M.F.A. from Cornell, where he lectured for two years. Friedman's poetry has appeared in *The New York Times*, *Parnassus*, *POETRY*, *Yale Review*, and other publications. He received a Ruth Lilly Fellowship in 2012 and was a Wallace Stegner fellow from 2014 to 2016. Friedman currently works as a Jones lecturer in poetry at Stanford.

Roni Fuller lived in Brooktondale, NY, for over 35 years. He currently resides in Ithaca. He has published three volumes of poetry with Visa Periodista in Ithaca.

Alice Fulton lived in Ithaca from 1980 to 1982 while she was working toward an M.F.A. at Cornell. Upon completing the degree, she spent a winter in Provincetown, then moved to Michigan where she lived for the next 19 years. In 2002, she accepted a teaching position at Cornell and returned to Ithaca, where she still lives. She is the author of numerous poetry collections, including *Barely Composed* (2015). www.alicefulton.com.

Mary Gardner has lived in Skaneateles, NY, since 1999 in a semi-rural, lakefront community. She is active in professional organizations in Central New York and is a frequent subscriber to cultural and artistic events. Her first chapbook, *When All Danger of Frost Is Past* (2015) reflects this lifestyle.

Christine Gelineau's latest full-length collection is *Crave* (2016). Other books include *Appetite for the Divine* (2010) and *Remorseless Loyalty* (2006). She won the Robert McGovern Prize and the Richard Snyder Prize. Gelineau teaches at Binghamton University where she is Associate Director of the Center for Writers. She also teaches in the low-res M.F.A. Program at Wilkes University. She and her husband live on a farm where they raise Morgan horses.

Kathleen Gemmell is the author of *A Common Bond* (1976) and has published in poetry magazines in the U.S., Ireland, and Peru, and in several broadside series. She has lived and written poetry in many places, from Finland to Ireland, from Washington, D.C. to Tallahassee, from

New York to Paris, from Arizona to Wyoming, and from San Francisco to Scotland.

Mary Gilliland's poetry has been awarded prizes nationally and internationally. She resides in Ithaca, New York, where she was formerly Director of Cornell's Writing Walk-In Service and taught writing. Among her singular accomplishments are a poetry workshop at Namgyal, the Dalai Lama's personal monastery in North America, and the civic service of preventing Ithaca from paving its 3-mile woodland South Hill Recreation Way. Mary has embarked on the poetry memoir *We Are All Immortals.*

Laura Glenn's poetry collection *I Can't Say I'm Lost* appeared in 2008. Her work has appeared widely, including *Antioch Review*, *Boulevard*, *Epoch*, *Massachusetts Review*, and *Poetry*. Her chapbook, *When the Ice Melts*, is forthcoming. Glenn is a Pushcart nominee, recipient of a CAP fellowship in poetry and a grant from AQE Ventures. Also a visual artist and freelance editor, she lives in Ithaca.

Jack Goldman is the owner of the Bookery, in Ithaca, which he began in 1975.

John Grau is a retired journalist, having worked for the *Post-Standard* in Syracuse from 1981 to 2007. He and his wife were relative newlyweds when they moved from New Jersey to Central New York. Since 1995, they have lived in a 160-year-old farmhouse near Skaneateles. From 1989 through 1991, he attended part-time the undergraduate Writing Arts Program at SUNY College at Oswego, where he studied poetry and fiction-writing under then department chair Lewis Turco. He is a member of the Skaneateles Writers' Group.

Andrei Guruianu lived and worked in upstate New York for more than a decade. In 2006 he first taught at Ithaca College, and since then he has regarded the area as his spiritual home. Although he works in New York City now and lives in Pennsylvania, he comes back to the hills and lakes of Ithaca several times a year for readings and writing workshops.

Tom Hall has lived in many places—most transformative was two years at Navajo Community College (now Diné College) in NE Arizona at Tsaile. There he set off on a career in anthropology and sociology, and began lifelong hobbies reading the Beat writers, poetry, especially Gary

Snyder, and Taoism and Zen. After his teaching years, he and his wife settled in Ithaca, where is learning how to be retired.

Paul Hamill retired from Ithaca College in 2011 after 25 years as an administrator and adjunct teacher of literature. He was a founding board member of both the Tompkins Country Arts Partnership and Ithaca City of Asylum. His most recent poetry collection is *Meeting the Minotaur* (2010). He was the Tompkins County Poet Laureate in 2008-09.

Lisa Harris came to the Finger Lakes, Keuka Lake, as a child with her extended family. When Jeff Spence and she decided to marry, he lived in the Adirondacks and she lived in coastal Georgia, and so they picked Ithaca and lived there from 1984 until 2013. She currently lives in Butler, PA. Her recent novels are *Geechie Girls* and *Allegheny Dream*.

Roger Hecht lives in the Finger Lakes Region. He earned his Ph.D. in English from Syracuse University and his M.F.A. in Poetry from the University of Arizona, where he helped to run the Among Other Things Reading Series and served as Director of the Tucson Poetry Festival. His work has appeared in *Zoomoozophone*, *The Otter*, *Prick of the Spindle*, *Diagram*, *Denver Quarterly*, and is forthcoming in *Arachne* and *Undertow Tanka Review*. His first full collection, *Talking Pictures*, was published by Cervena Barva Press.

Roald Hoffmann has lived in Ithaca for 51 years. He has taught and done research at Cornell for all that time. Poetry has been with him since college at Columbia, and a course by Mark Van Doren. But he began to write poetry seriously only in midlife, and in doing so was encouraged by Archie Ammons. He has had book-length selections of his poetry translated into Russian and Spanish, and has published widely here. He also writes plays.

Elizabeth Holmes has lived in Ithaca for the past 31 years, having come here originally for graduate school in poetry at Cornell. She has published two collections of poetry with Carnegie Mellon University Press, as well as many poems in journals and three novels for children. She works at Cornell University.

Gail Holst-Warhaft is an adjunct professor in the Departments of Comparative Literature and Biological and Environmental Engineering and a member of the Graduate Field of Music at Cornell University where she is also director of the Mediterranean Studies Initiative in the

Institute for European Studies. Other areas of interest are Modern Greek literature and music. She was Poet Laureate of Tompkins County for 2011 and 2012. Her many books include the poetry collection, *Penelope's Confession.*

Jack Hopper writes poetry chiefly, and edits scholarly material as well as fiction. He has published three collections of poetry, most recently *Doubles: Poems 1995-2012* (Cayuga Lake Books). He founded *Works: A Quarterly of Writing* (1967-1974). An Ithacan since 2005, he is one of the Aladdin poetry group and the Ekphrastic Four. He is serving his second term as poet laureate of Tompkins County, NY. www.johnhopperauthor.com

Eric Machan Howd has lived in the Finger Lakes region since 1986 when he entered Ithaca College in Music Education. After graduating as an English major, with a Writing minor, he settled in Ithaca to raise a family with poet Katharyn Howd Machan. He currently works at Binghamton University as the Director of Instructional Design in its Center for Learning and Teaching and he also teaches professional writing in Ithaca College's Department of Writing.

Rachael Ikins was born near Skaneateles Lake and raised there. Growing up with a wild, solitary space to play in the woods, water and fields influenced her irrevocably as a writer. Six chapbooks of her poetry have been published and she has been awarded many prizes for her poetry as well as for her prose. She is also a visual artist. She lives in Baldwinsville near the Seneca River. www.about.me/rachaelz.

Sarah Jefferis is an author, editor, and mentor. Her writing consultant business, Write Now, offers writing workshops, copy-editing, and public speaking services to writers. She also works as a writing consultant at the Office of Academic Diversity Initiatives at Cornell University. Her most recent book of poetry, *What Enters the Mouth*, is forthcoming in 2017, and she is completing her first novel and a collection of essays on single motherhood. She lives in Ithaca, NY with her two daughters.

Michael Jennings came to Central New York in 1972 as a graduate student in Creative Writing at Syracuse University, living for the last 33 years overlooking Otisco Lake with his wife, poet Suzan Shane. He taught for several decades in the New York State Poets-in-the-Schools Program, serving week-long residencies in public schools from Oswego to Binghamton and from Oneida to Waterloo; and for the last 25 years he has taught a variety of English courses at Cayuga Community College.

Atiya Jordan presently lives in Queens, New York, her home for 21 years. She graduated from Wells College in Aurora in 2016. The Finger Lakes region opened her eyes to a larger world than what she had been used to, and her writing became stronger, ultimately inspiring her English thesis to explore the brown body in nature. Her connection to the Finger Lakes, to Cayuga Lake and the waterfalls she has visited could never be severed.

Julie Kane was an undergraduate at Cornell University 1970-1974 during which time she wrote both of the poems republished here. One of Anne Sexton's graduate poetry students at Boston University, Kane has published widely. She moved to Louisiana after marrying a native, then stayed after the marriage ended, completed her PhD, and until recently was a professor of English at Northwestern State University. She was the 2011-2013 Louisiana Poet Laureate. www.juliekanepoet.com

Emma Karnes has lived in Ithaca, NY, since starting high school three years ago. When she was little her family had a house on Cayuga Lake where she spent many wonderful summers.

Douglas Keating has lived and taught in Ithaca, New York for the past 30 years. He came to this region for schooling but began an education. His work as an artist, musician, and teacher has been influenced deeply by the people, the land, and the tempo of life in the Finger Lakes. He will be forever grateful to the teachers, friends, and community that make their lives here: they have helped him to gain whatever footing he might have.

Kathleen Kramer moved to the beautiful Finger Lakes region from Long Island 23 years ago. Retired now from her position as Library Director for the Boyce Thompson Institute, Kathy and her husband Jack love their home in Newfield, overlooking a valley of lush woodlands and farms. It was in the Finger Lakes that Kathy's poetry life truly took root. Her books of poetry include *Boiled Potato Blues* and *Planting Wild Grapes*, published in 2016.

C. Kubasta was a student at Wells College in the late 1990s where she studied under Bruce Bennett, and Aurora and Wells will always feel like home to her. She currently lives in Wisconsin, teaching English and cultural studies at Marian University. She is the author of two poetry chapbooks, *A Lovely Box* and *&s,* as well as a full-length collection, *All Beautiful & Useless.* Her next book, *Of Covenants,* is forthcoming in 2017. www.ckubasta.com

Michelle Lee went to school at Wells College and graduated last year after staring at the lake from her room and watching sunsets on walks to the dining hall or dorms. She moved to New York City this fall to continue studying creative writing at The New School. She doesn't think she could live anywhere that doesn't have a body of water near.

Jay Leeming is the author of *Dynamite on a China Plate* (2006) and *Miracle Atlas* (2011). His poems have appeared in such magazines as *Ploughshares, The Gettysburg Review, Rattapallax,* and *Pleiades.* He has taught poetry workshops throughout the United States and abroad, and is the recipient of a Creative Writing Fellowship from the National Endowment for the Arts. He teaches poetry in his hometown Ithaca, NY, through the Green Horse Poetry School that he founded in 2016.

David Lehman has lived in Ithaca since 1980—full-time for many years and now mainly during summers and occasional weekends in fall or spring. A widely published poet as well as a critic, he is also the editor of the annual series, *The Best American Poetry.* He is on the core faculty of the graduate writing programs at the New School and New York University. www.poets.org/poetsorg/poet/david-lehman

Stephen Lewandowski has lived most of his life in the Finger Lakes region of upstate New York. He has worked professionally and as a volunteer for many environmental groups of the area. He considers his poetry "the other side" of that same coin. During his days as a student, he studied literature, philosophy and folk culture. Since 1974, he has published 14 books of poetry and edited other literary projects in connection with White Pine Press.

Dick Lourie lived in Ithaca in the early '60s and in the mid-'70s, teaching as an adjunct at Ithaca College and working with elementary school children. He is a founding editor (1966) of Hanging Loose Press. Since 1981 he has lived near Boston with his wife, filmmaker Abby Freedman. His latest poetry collection, *If the Delta Was the Sea*, focuses on the Mississippi Delta and his experiences there as both a poet and blues saxophone player. www.hangingloosepress.com

Katharyn Howd Machan has made her home in Ithaca since May of 1975. Since 1977 she has taught in the Department of Writing at Ithaca College, where she is now a full professor. She served as Tompkins County's first poet laureate from 2002-2004. She is the author of several collections, including *Redwing: Voices from 1888,* and the chapbook *H.*

Ruth Mahr arrived in Ithaca by train in September 1958 to attend graduate school at Cornell University. She's still here! Ruth married and had three children in Ithaca. She taught economics at various colleges and universities in the area, and, after a semester in Prague in 1992, she retired from teaching and returned to an early love: writing. Much of the inspiration for her poems is derived from the way Ruth experiences the natural world.

Caroline Manring grew up in Skaneateles, NY, and now lives in Ithaca. Her book *Manual for Extinction* won the National Poetry Review Prize in 2012. Her work has appeared in *Colorado Review, Conduit, Drunken Boat, Jubilat, Seneca Review, Sixth Finch, Vese Daily*, and elsewhere. She is a graduate of Cornell and the Iowa Writers' Workshop.

Fran Markover has long held a connection to the Finger Lakes. After graduating from Ithaca College in 1967, she would leave for other locations and always return to the Finger Lakes where she has lived for over 30 years. She is married to a "townie," works in the community as a psychotherapist and addictions counselor and can't imagine residing elsewhere. Her poetry chapbook is *History's Trail.*

Katherine May has lived in the Finger Lakes for most of her life, in Ithaca from 1987 to 2002 and in Trumansburg from 2002 to the present. The Finger Lakes is her home, no matter where she may wander, and she loves the beauty of the rolling hills, and the lakes and the old farms dotting the landscape.

David McAleavey's Ithaca roots go deep. He first came to Ithaca as an undergraduate at Cornell and then returned as a graduate student. He has three degrees from Cornell (B.A., M.F.A., Ph.D.). He and his wife Kathy Perry now live where they raised their children in the part of Virginia that originally formed the District of Columbia. A professor of English at George Washington University in D.C., he is the author of numerous books of poetry.

Joyce Holmes McAllister was born when her parents lived on West Hill in Ithaca, NY, overlooking Cayuga Lake. She was raised in this area, graduating from Dryden High School and Ithaca College. After spending several years in New York City, she returned to Ithaca, where she was employed at Cornell University for thirty years. She is now retired, still living in and enjoying the Finger Lakes area.

Kenneth McClane has lived in Ithaca since 1969 when he came to Cornell as an undergraduate. He remained in Ithaca for graduate work and then taught English and creative writing at Cornell for 37 years. He is the author of seven poetry collections, including *A Tree Beyond Telling: Selected Poems*. His creative non-fiction has been collected in two books, *Walls: Essays 1985-1990* and *Color: Essays on Race, Family, and History*. He lives on West Hill with his wonderful wife, Rochelle.

Bridget Meeds now lives a block from the banks of Six Mile Creek, which empties into Cayuga Lake, which she chose as her own when she moved to Ithaca in 1987. For a single year in the early 90s, she lived on a cliff above the Irish Sea, and later, a stone's throw to the banks of the Lagan River in Belfast. She grew up a few miles from Onondaga Lake, a wounded body of water, still her omphalos.

Raymond J. Metrulis became a poet after studying with Mark McCloskey at SUNY Cortland and then with Norman Dubie at the Iowa Writer's Workshop. He wanted to teach, but instead worked as a driver for florists in Manhattan for 35 years. His poems have appeared in *The Nation*, *Rolling Stone*, *The Grapevine*, *Oasis D'Neon*, *Redtape*, and *Jane*. Retired, he lives in Ithaca. The poem he's working on now is called "A List of Words I Cannot Say in Ithaca."

Jerry Mirskin settled in Ithaca in 1992 and has been here ever since. He has swum across Cayuga Lake and ridden his bicycle (many times) around all of the Finger Lakes. He has stayed for weeks at a time on a small boat on Cayuga, and has worked at Ithaca College for 24 years. Most of his adventures as a father and husband have taken place here. He is the author of several poetry collections. www.jerrymirskin.org

Robert Morgan has since 1970 taught in the English Department at Cornell University. Poet, novelist, essayist, and historian, he is the author of many books. His most recent collection of poetry is *Dark Energy,* and his latest novel is *Chasing the North Star.* Originally from

Hendersonville, North Carolina, he writes of the Finger Lakes: "What better place for working could a poet such as myself find?" www.robert-morgan.com

Benjamin Mueller and his wife moved from the Hudson Valley to Ithaca, New York, with their twins when they were a year old in order to be closer to family. They fell in love with the culture and natural beauty the area offers and have quickly put their roots down.

Becca Myers has lived in the Finger Lakes region for almost two years now. She and her husband moved up here from Georgia when she was nine months pregnant, so her first memories of Cayuga Lake are of doing calisthenics on the shore and trying to will the baby into coming (he was of course 10 days late). She taught this past year at Wells College.

Howard Nelson has lived in the Finger Lakes region for 45 years, almost all of them in Scipio, part-way between Auburn and Ithaca. He currently serves on the town board of Scipio. He has taught for many years at Cayuga Community College, where he was recently named Professor Emeritus. He didn't expect to stay in the same place and job when he came here, but he did. www.howardnelsonpoet.com

Mary Beth O'Connor settled in the Finger Lakes in the early 80's. In Ithaca, she delivered newspapers, worked for a Cornell professor who was developing low cost solar projects for developing countries, cooked at a fraternity, did a stint as a photographer, wrote...and then went back to school and worked toward her Ph.D. in English at SUNY Binghamton. Upon graduating, she began teaching at Ithaca College, and has just retired after twenty years and taken up painting.

Stanley J. O'Connor lives in Ithaca, NY, and he taught at Cornell for many years. His love for the Finger Lakes began as a child when he spent summers on his grandparents' farm.

Edward Ormondroyd has written more than a dozen children's books (among them—*David and the Phoenix, Time at the Top, All in Good Time, Theodore*) while serving as a librarian, first in California and then in Ithaca at the Finger Lakes Library System. When he retired and the children had left home, he and his wife Joan moved to Trumansburg, again into a home Edward had designed and built. Although he is no longer writing children's books he enjoys "dabbling" with poetry when not practicing the piano or cultivating his veggie garden.

Tish Pearlman is a poet and broadcast journalist from Manhattan Beach, California. She is host of the award-winning public radio interview show "Out of Bounds." Her chapbook *The Fix Is In,* which re-told her near-death heart surgery experience, was published in 2012. Her newest collection, *Afterlife* was published in 2014. She was 2013-2014 Poet Laureate of Tompkins County, NY. Pearlman lives in Ithaca, NY. www.outofboundsradioshow.com

Anna Pensky was born in Ithaca and has lived in the Finger Lakes region for 18 of her 20 years—two years she spent away in England. In addition to writing poetry, she practices digital drawing and collage, printmaking, and prose fiction. In the future she hopes to finish her B.A. and attend Cornell University as a culinary student, and one day to open an art café. www.society6.com/mothchildren.

Stephen Poleskie's writing has appeared in literary journals in Australia, Czech Republic, Germany, India, Italy, Mexico, the UK, and the USA. He has published seven books of fiction. His artworks are in the Metropolitan Museum and the Museum of Modern Art in New York, and The Tate Gallery and Victoria and Albert Museum in London, among others. Poleskie is a professor emeritus at Cornell University and lives in Ithaca, NY, with his wife Jeanne Mackin. www.StephenPoleskie.com

Lynn Powell lived in Ithaca from 1977-1979, where she received her M.F.A. from Cornell University and then taught for a year at Cornell and Ithaca College. She has published two books of poetry (*Old & New Testaments* and *The Zones of Paradise)* and a book of nonfiction (*Framing Innocence)*. She has lived in Oberlin, Ohio, since 1990, where she teaches at Oberlin College and is Director of *Oberlin WITS* (the Writers-in-the-Schools program).

Frank W. Robinson has lived in Ithaca since 1992 as director of the Johnson Museum at Cornell (1992-2011) and as a consultant on museums since then, and a volunteer at Cinemapolis and Cornell. He resides at Kendal at Ithaca.

Bertha Rogers lives in the western Catskills but has spent a great deal of time in the Finger Lakes Region and, as founding director of Bright Hill Press & Literary Center, has hosted many poets and writers from the Finger Lakes in their Word Thursdays reading series she's curated since 1992. www.bertharogers.com

Dan Rosenberg is the author of *cadabra* (2015) and *The Crushing Organ* (2012), which won the American Poetry Journal Book Prize. He has also written two chapbooks, *A Thread of Hands* (2010) and *Thigh's Hollow* (2015), which won the Omnidawn Poetry Chapbook Contest, and he co-translated Miklavž Komelj's *Hippodrome* (2016). Rosenberg teaches literature and creative writing at Wells College and co-edits *Transom*. www.danrosenberg.us

Harry Rosenberg has been a resident at Kendal at Ithaca for nine years.

Carol Rubenstein arrived in Ithaca, NY, in November 1989. It felt very cold, as she had recently been in Sarawak, East Malaysia, Borneo. She had previously done research there to collect and translate oral poetry of the Dayaks. With an NEA grant for Literary Translation she later returned. In 2004-2005 with the help of a small grant from the Saltonstall Foundation, she visited Poland three times to experience something of Auschwitz and other such places. She is now developing a manuscript based on those experiences.

Leeny Sack lived in Ithaca, NY, from 2002-2008, then in Boulder, CO, from 2008-2016, and resides in Ithaca now again, home again. www.leenysack.com

Mary Michael Shelley, cover artist, writes, "I am commonly referred to as a folk or self-taught artist. My subject matter usually is of places and feelings that are important to me, and I think of my artwork as a 'picture diary.' My work is carved on one-inch-thick pine boards, then painted with acrylics and gold leafed. It can be found in the collections of the American Folk Art Museum, Fenimore Art Museum and the National Museum of Women and the Arts. I carve every summer Saturday at the Ithaca Farmers' Market." www.maryshelleyfolkart.com

Daphne Solá lives in Ithaca; she is a pianist, a printmaker, and owns an art gallery. She and her husband, a professor at Cornell, moved here to escape life in New York City. She has studied book-making at Wells College Summer Book Arts Institute and produced artist-books as well as several chapbooks of her poems. When asked about the moves from one art form to another, she says, "It's really all the same thing."

William Stratton was born in Norwich, NY and currently lives and writes in Colchester, Vermont. He teaches poetry and writing at Burlington College and St. Michaels College. His first full-length collection of poetry, *Under The Water Was Stone* (2014) was nominated for the Kate Tufts Discovery award and the Eugene Paul Nassar Award. His second book *These Things Too Have Shape* was released in January of 2016. His work has so far been nominated five times for the Pushcart Prize.

Sarah Sutro's poetry book *Études* was recently published. A student at Cornell from 1968-1972, she then studied at Yale and University of the Arts in London. In 1976 she returned to Ithaca for four years, teaching at Cornell, Ithaca High School, and Ithaca College, with a studio at Sheldon Court in Collegetown. She now lives in North Adams, MA, where she writes for *American Arts Quarterly*. www.sarahsutro.com

Judy Swann has lived on West Hill longer than she lived in her hometown. When her son was five, they painted the house a brilliant blue with red trim, like Frida Kahlo's *casa azul*. When he was a teenager, they added solar panels. When Judy dies she wants to be buried at Greensprings, and she wants a big party with lots of drinking and bad behavior, as if they were in New Orleans.

Carol Whitlow has lived in the hamlet of Varna for 35 years. She enjoys hiking the gorge trails, finding wildflowers and summer flowers at Cornell Plantations, kayaking and canoeing the lakes and streams and photographing the beauty of the area.

Fred A. Wilcox is a journalist, fiction writer, and poet. He has written extensively about the use of chemical warfare in Vietnam, and is a veterans' advocate. His novel, *Tommy Machin's Vow*, was published in 2016 by Cayuga Lake Books.

Kidd Williams lives in Bath and has published poetry and fiction. Most proudly, she has twice had her poems selected by the Poetry Posts project for summer displays in Elmira parks. Kidd lives with a wife and two dogs. (Kidd is a pen-name for her real first name, now Joy.)

Greg Wooster came to Ithaca in 1985 to work at Cornell and has lived in Tompkins County ever since. He met his beautiful wife while on a ski outing at Hammond Hill State Forest, and they have a wonderful daughter. For him, poetry comes at moments of inspiration and cannot be forced on command. He currently lives in Danby, adjacent to Sweedler Preserve and Lick Brook Gorge for which he is a trail steward.

THE CAYUGA LAKE BOOKS EDITORS

Rhian Ellis is a writer living in Ithaca, NY. Her novel, *After Life*, was published by Viking Press in 2000 and was included in Nancy Pearl's *Book Lust Rediscoveries* series in 2012. Her stories have appeared in literary journals including *Epoch* and the anthology *New Stories from the South*. She holds an MFA from the University of Montana and an MA from SUNY Cortland. www.rhianellis.com.

Peter Fortunato has lived in Ithaca for most of his life. A poet, a visual artist, the author of fiction and non-fiction, a cofounder of Cayuga Lake Books, Peter taught writing at Cornell University and Ithaca College for many years and also spent four years teaching at Weill Cornell Medical College in Qatar. He is a practitioner of complementary alternative medicine, specializing in hypnosis. www.peterfortunato.wordpress.com.

Jack Hopper is a writer, chiefly of poetry, editor for the academic publisher AMS Press, and a cofounder of Cayuga Lake Books. He has published three books of poetry, most recently *Doubles: Poems 1995 – 2012*. He founded and edited *Works: A Quarterly of Writing*. An Ithacan for the past eleven years, he has read on local radio and at libraries in the area, and is a member of the Aladdin poetry group and The Ekphrastic Four. He is the current Poet Laureate for Tompkins County, New York. www.johnhopperauthor.com.

Edward Hower, an Ithaca resident since 1974, has published eleven books, most recently, *What Can You Do: Personal Essays and Travel Writing,* and *Slick,* a novel. His work has appeared in *The New York Times, Atlantic Monthly, Smithsonian, American Scholar, Epoch,* and elsewhere. He has been awarded two Fulbright fellowships to India and writing grants from the National Endowment for the Arts and the New York State Council on the Arts. He is a cofounder of Cayuga Lake Books. www.edwardhower.com.

MaryBeth Cooper is an intern at Cayuga Lake Books. Originally from South Carolina, she is a senior at Ithaca College majoring in Cinema and Photography and minoring in Writing. She has published two photographs, *Ephemeral* and *Old Friends*, in IC's *Stillwater Magazine* (2016). After graduation, she plans to enroll in an M.F.A. program in fiction and to continue writing about dysfunctional characters or the next thing that comes to mind

ACKNOWLEDGMENTS

Diane Ackerman's "We Die" was previously published in her book *I Praise My Destroyer*.

Nick Admussen's "From Us and Back In" originally appeared in *Seneca Review*.

Katherine Anderson's "Rush" was first published in *Hotel Amerika*.

Emily Benson-Scott's "The Problem with Paradise" originally appeared in *Nimrod*.

Cory Brown's poems "Autumn Lament" and "Memento Mori" were first published in his book *What May Be Lost*.

Alex Chertok's "The question" was first published in *Willow Springs*.

Nancy Vieira Couto's "Just when She Thought It Was Safe" first appeared in *Prairie Schooner*.

Ann Day's poems "We Have Saved What We Can" and "Old War" were first published in her book *We Have Saved What We Can*. Her artwork first appeared in her book *Poetry & Penwork*.

Nancy Flynn's poems "Meridian" and "Tide Table" first appeared in *Verseweavers*.

Peter Fortunato's "*from* Letters to Tiohero" was previously published in his book *Late Morning: New and Selected Poems*.

Nicholas Friedman's "As Is" first appeared in *Poetry* and "The Illusionist" was published in *The Yale Review*.

Roni Fuller's "Persistence" was first published in his book *God's Breath*.

Alice Fulton's poems "Because We Never Practiced with the Escape Chamber" and "Still World Nocturne" were previously published in her book *Barely Composed*.

Katharyn Howd Machan's "The Beets Poem" originally appeared in *Hanging Loose*, and "An Account of My Disappearances" was first published in *Chautauqua Journal*.

David McAleavey's "While holding obsidian from Milos" was previously published in his book *While Holding Obsidian* and "Observing dusk at the Warren family camp. . ." was previously published in his book *Rock Taught*.

Joyce Holmes McAllister's "Pilgrim's Progress" originally appeared in *Comstock Review*.

Kenneth McClane's "An Edge of Thanks" and "The Butterfly" were previously published in his book *Take Five: Collected Poems, 1971 - 1988*.

Raymond J. Metrulis's "April" was first published in *Stranded*, and "Leo Stonecutter" was published in *The Nation*.

Jerry Mirskin's "Rock and Water" and "Seasonal Work" were previously published in his book, *Picture A Gate Hanging Open and Let that Gate be the Sun*.

Robert Morgan's "Yellow" was previously published in his book *At the Edge of the Orchard Country,* and "Purple Asters" was previously published in his book *Sigodlin*.

Tish Pearlman's "In the Distance" was previously published in her book *Afterlife*.

Stephen Poleskie's "One More Time" was previously published as a *Poem in Your Pocket* by the Tompkins County Public Library, and "Blue Sky" was published by the Loughborough College of Art and Design, UK.

Lynn Powell's "Love Poem from the Wrong Side of the Rain" first appeared in *Shenandoah,* and "July's Proverb" first appeared in *Rivendell*.

Dan Rosenberg's "Best Friends" was previously published in *jubilat*.

Also available from Cayuga Lake Books

FROM THE FINGER LAKES:
A PROSE ANTHOLOGY

Published in 2015, this anthology immediately became a regional favorite. Ask for it at your local book store or order it on line from amazon.com or barnesandnoble.com. A fascinating collection, it features memoir, fiction, essays and articles by 44 authors—ages 23 to 93.

"The list of outright professional writers in the area is shockingly long, given the density of places like Ithaca and Trumansburg... What may be more impressive is the number of people who also write, and very well—enough to make you wonder how exceptional they must be as the lawyers, carpenters, anthropologists, pastors, mathematicians, librarians, artists, and teachers that they are by day."

—Ryan Chamberlin, *Ithaca Times*

To learn more about all of our publications, visit our website
cayugalakebooks.com

Made in the USA
Columbia, SC
03 March 2021